Potted Meat and Politics

*Why Rednecks Will
Save America*

by
Steve Nelson

authorHOUSE®

AuthorHouse™
1663 Liberty Drive, Suite 200
Bloomington, IN 47403
www.authorhouse.com
Phone: 1-800-839-8640

First published by AuthorHouse 1/3/2011

ISBN: 978-1-4389-1482-4 (sc)
ISBN: 978-1-4389-1483-1 (dj)

Printed in the United States of America

Any people depicted in stock imagery provided by Thinkstock are models, and such images are being used for illustrative purposes only. Certain stock imagery © Thinkstock.

This book is printed on acid-free paper.

Contents

Preface

Like most Americans who work for a living, I have no desire to waste my free time publicly proclaiming envy for the things others may have that I desire. Yes, rather than waste my time trying to persuade politicians to steal from others on my behalf, I prefer to spend my time thinking of how to earn what it is that I desire. While protests and government programs may be the preferred methods of the less than mediocre, they are no substitute for self-esteem attained from having actually accomplished something. So, when some dumbass or group of dumbasses decides that they are the arbiters of what is fair, I tend to get a little worked-up. Just how worked-up, usually depends on how much more they are trying to take from me.

That said, it's not just the dumbasses that are bothering me; it's also the apathetic and disinterested who piss-me-off. Whether you are a concerned conservative, liberal or libertarian, the... "I don't give a damn crowd," has a tendency to piss off all who are concerned, regardless of political affiliation. Still, while the apathetic and disinterested can be annoying with such comments as... "All politicians are alike!" or "My vote doesn't matter anyway!" they don't even come close to the Left's ability to rile me up. Besides, I'll take harmless inane platitudes over flagrantly destructive stupidity any day.

Whether you're an idiot or an apathetic fool; should you exhibit your stupidity in my presence, I'm not one to usually let it go. I consider it my duty—depending on the severity of stupidity exhibited—to educate the ignorant. Sadly though, not everyone is appreciative of my selflessness and desire to educate, especially the Left. Moreover, the only thing I've yet to receive for my gratuitous compassion is the befuddled... 'I-don't-give-a-damn' shrug of the shoulders or someone's middle finger. Given that I've been unable to convince many of their ignorance or stupidity, I've resigned myself to believe that the apathetic are simply indifferent fools and the Left incapable of common-sense.

While there is not much a liberal can say or do to shock me these days, I must admit that I have been taken aback by the heightened fervor of their anti-Americanism post 9-11. After 9-11, most Americans managed to put aside their political differences for the betterment of the Country, but not the hard-Left. A new war—especially one led by a Republican—was all that they needed to revitalize an anti-American movement that had been languishing since the early eighties. Still, had it not been for the dress wearing, pig hating, female bashing, murderous psychopaths of Islam, millions of Americans may never have known just how far many on the Left were willing to go to further their social and economic schemes.

To all variants of the Democratic Party: leftists, liberals, socialists, progressives, anarchists and communists alike, you will no doubt—in your typical narrow spectrum of thought—

try to tag me with one or more of your many idiotic labels for the content of this book. For this reason, a quick lesson may be in order. First of all, true conservatism, individualism or capitalism has nothing to do with fascism, racism, imperialism or militarism and everything to do with liberty.

For anyone who thinks otherwise, I'll assume the Left's preferred method of teaching (brainwashing) has already been successful. Secondly, most conservatives are not up-tight people intent on ruling by theocracy. In fact, it has been my experience that most conservatives are laid-back civil libertarians with no greater desire other than to be self-made capitalists living in a society governed by an unobtrusive government. As for myself, I'm about as laid back as a blue-tick hound on a hot summer day. Believe me when I tell you that I wouldn't give a rat's ass about the stupid things liberals do or believe in, if it didn't affect my pocket-book or individual liberty.

Because I believe that life, liberty and capitalism are so important to America's success, one of the goals of this book is to prove that some Americans aren't really true Americans. Being the protagonist that I am, I know that such a statement will be challenged and that I will need facts to support my contention. For this reason, I will ask and answer the obvious question: What is it that makes one a true American? Now, before you arrive at the same undeniable conclusion that I have, you will have to accept that there is a distinction between an American by law and an American philosophically.

Though it is possible to be either one or the other, to be a true American one must be both. For instance, a person born in America may be an American by law, but what if this same person believed in and advocated communism? Would he then be an American philosophically? It is my contention that he would not. To be an American philosophically, your principles must be founded in the U.S. Constitution as it relates to individual liberty. Any form of collectivist ideology—such as communism, socialism, or fascism is anti-Constitution, and thus anti-American.

By way of this simple line of logic, I have concluded that before one can be considered a true American, one must be both an American by law and philosophically. Now, you may question whether or not I have the right to judge whether someone is a true American or not, and I certainly wouldn't argue with your right to do so, but to disagree with my supposition would prove my point all together. Not even the Left is stupid enough to claim that socialism, in all its variations, is philosophically American, much less an ideal espoused by our founders. During your read, you will learn that there have been several events in my life that have led me to this and other simple conclusions. The following story is just one of many.

On June 1, 1999, my wife was a stewardess onboard a commercial flight that crashed on landing late at night in Little Rock, Arkansas, killing the Captain and 10 passengers. By around 10:00 a.m. that morning, I was by her side in the hospital. Fortunately, her injuries were not life threatening and all that she lost was her luggage and will to fly. Since she was without additional clothing and some essential sundry items, she asked if I could go out and buy her some new clothes and make-up before our car ride back to Dallas. Though I would have preferred to fly back, I was the considerate husband and respected her newfound apprehension to flying.

Being also the sensitive fellow that I am, I agreed to go shopping and found the nearest store possible. As you might have guessed, it was a Wal-Mart. I hadn't been in the store for more than a minute when I overheard a little boy ask his mother, a woman of considerable expanse, "Momma, why ain't he gotta get walk?" To which she responded, "Billy Bob, you bess shut up 'fore I whip your ass!" Now, granted, I was in a Wal-Mart, where such an occurrence between mother and child is probably not an uncommon event. But, what puzzled me was the manner in which the child had asked the question: "Momma, why ain't he gotta get walk?" Nobody "gets walk!" Hell, I'm half Redneck and I had no idea of what he meant.

Even after I had changed course to place greater distance between myself and Momma's rendition of a plumber taken leave of his suspenders, I couldn't help but wonder what Billy Bob could have meant. Then it came to me; the boy's little brother was getting a ride in the shopping cart, while he was forced to follow behind Momma and stare up at what must have looked like the largest sack of potatoes he ever did saw. I'm not kidding, this is a true story. Aside from the obvious comedic material this encounter offered, it got me to thinking about that poor little guy who had to "get walk."

Though he could not have known it at the time, Billy Bob had learned two of life's most valuable lessons: 1) you can't always get what you want and 2) life isn't always fair. That said I couldn't really see the harm in Momma letting him ride in the cart. What was an extra 50 or so pounds? It wasn't as though she couldn't have used the exercise. Was she actually trying to teach him life's valuable lessons, or was she just being lazy? Considering her size and inability to teach her child proper English, I think it must have been the latter. No, I know it was the latter.

It seems that on this day, Momma and I were predestined to meet again, as Momma, Billy Bob, and little brother (never caught his name) entered the checkout line next to me. Now that Momma and brood were in such close proximity to the strategically placed candy rack at the checkout lane, I fully expected the next conflict to be over multiple requests for candy. Unfortunately, it was worse. The boys didn't have to beg for candy, because Momma reached over with her pudgy little fingers and grabbed a handful of candy bars. By this time all I could do was shake my head in disgust, and as though to piss me off further, she had the nerve to squint her eyes at me as if she knew I was judging her to be a horrible mother. Well, I was, but that's not the point.

She might as well have poked me in the eye with a stick, because what happened next just about had me screaming, "Momma, why aint she gotta get work?" This poor excuse of a mother pulled out what appeared to be foreign currency and paid the cashier. I asked my cashier in a subdued voice, (so as not to rile the beast), 'What is that she's paying with?' After looking over his shoulder he turned and answered, "Oh, that's welfare money!" I countered, "Welfare money...you mean food stamps, right?" "Yeah, food stamps," he answered.

After witnessing that exchange I had no doubt in my mind as to which political party Momma supported, even if she didn't vote. You see, Momma is just one example of the anti-American. Although it is unlikely that Momma is even capable of defining socialism or communism, she is an unwitting proponent of these similar anti-American philosophies. If you think that I am just being mean, I don't care, because my tax dollars afford that lazy good-for-nothing horrible mother the opportunity to sit around on her big butt doing nothing, and I'm sick of her, others like her, and her enablers (liberals). If you're wondering how I knew she was a Fat Lazy Liberal, that's easy; I profiled her.

While the Left is likely to pass this book off as the simple musings of a misguided Redneck, I prefer to think of it as more an affirmation of southern colloquial charm. Now, before you accept any characterization of me or of this book, I'd like to ask that you refrain from final judgment until you have completed the book. If I have not been able to convince you otherwise, then go ahead and judge me as you wish. Because odds are that if you find yourself in complete disagreement with me, I'll certainly be judging you as just another anti-American dumbass.

Chapter 1

Potted Meat and Politics

"Opportunity is missed by most people because it is dressed in overalls and looks like work." Thomas Edison

Though I have never been one to complain much about what was being served at the table, there was one particular food in the home that no matter how hard I tried, I just couldn't get beyond my initial gag reflex. Whether it was the gelatin like ooze at the top of every can or the eerie feeling I got from biting into it, I would cringe at its very sight. With such reactions, one might think that a little compassion would have been in order, but it didn't matter how much I protested, because this meat-by-product concoction could and did appear often as the main course for breakfast, lunch and dinner.

So, what is this culinary façade I speak of? This conglomeration of meat-by-products so heinous I wouldn't feed it to a communist on a bad day! SPAM, yes none other than SPAM. I know its

1

been credited with helping to feed the world during some pretty tough times and as even being a significant improvement over sea rations for our military, but I still think it should be relegated to pet food status. To this day I can't stand the stuff and should it ever appear at my table, I would consider it a personal affront to my dignity and as possible grounds for divorce.

Besides, if I have to eat meat out of a can, it's nothing but potted meat for me. I say hats off to the people at Armour Foods for this southern version of meat-by-product pâté. Anyone who can mix together the entrails of a cow, assorted pig parts and other meat byproducts with a little bit of spice to create a pâté that rivals the best of any European nation, deserves all the praise in the world. Not only is this stuff better than SPAM or snails, it beats the hell out of any goose liver or salmon pâté I've ever eaten and it keeps a hell of a lot longer too. Other than a pizza smothered in anchovies, I can't think of a better treat than potted meat on a saltine cracker. Even as I write this first chapter, I am partaking in that peculiar culinary delight that is potted meat.

In fact, did you know that even today, at full retail price, potted meat costs only about 29¢ a can? Try buying some sissy French brand of pâté for that. From what I can remember as a kid, potted meat was only about 15¢ a can and that was over 20 years ago. That's less than the average annual inflation rate of 3%. I tell you, you just can't beat it! Add some Ramen noodles at 19¢ a package and eight saltine crackers at about 10¢ and you've got a three-course meal for less than 60¢. If one does not require variety in their diet, that's less than a $1.80 for three squares a day. At these prices, not even a bum would find it difficult to feed himself after squeezing a couple bucks off some hapless liberal.

Now, you may be wondering what in the hell does potted meat have to do with politics. Well I'll tell you: nothing! It just happened to be what I was eating when I first became interested in politics. But, that was no real coincidence, because odds were that if I was snacking on something, it was usually potted meat and crackers. I've always loved the stuff and still do. You see, late one night I was eating some potted meat while flipping through the channels on the old cable box when I happened across CSPAN. I remember, because it was my senior year in high school.

No, I wasn't a geek, who preferred CSPAN to chasing girls on a Friday night; I just happened to be incapacitated at the time. While riding on the back of a three-wheeler, my leg was broken when a less-than-coordinated friend of mine decided to run into the biggest pine tree in the forest. As luck would have it, he walked away and I got a shattered leg. Having already spent a couple of weeks in what was to be a 5-month sentence with a cast from my crotch down to my toes, I hadn't much else to do other than watch TV. Rather than watch the latest T&A video on MTV for the 50th time, I stopped at CSPAN to hear what was so important so late into the night.

At first, I didn't know what was going on. There was this gray-haired dude on one side of the screen and a group of four or five others on the other side. I can't remember what the discussion was about, only that this lone gray-haired dude was making a lot of sense and was ripping the others apart with his wit and knowledge of history. I had always been extremely interested in the unabridged version of American history and considered myself a hardcore patriotic American, but something happened that night that got me hooked on politics. I remember that the following day, I tried to discuss what I'd seen the night before with some friends, but they just looked at me like I was goofy.

I may not have known it then, but I had definitely been bitten by the political bug. By the time I reached my early twenties I found myself following politics almost daily. Yes, I had become a political news junky. Though it wasn't until 1994, when Newt Gingrich and friends began pushing the "Contract with America" that I realized who that gray-haired dude was. As I began to pay closer attention to what was going on in Congress, I followed Newt's efforts closely and for a time thought he might be the one to pick-up where Reagan had left off. But, unfortunately it wasn't to be. Lacking Reagan's ability to bypass the press and take it directly to the people, Newt's image was quickly manipulated by the leftist press and he was soon forced out by a back-sliding Republican party.

Anyway, after years of reading various publications and listening to mainstream media outlets, I realized that most of the people I'd subjected myself to, didn't have a whole-hell-of-a-lot of common-sense. The things that most mainstream media outlets were writing and saying about America really pissed me off. I would get so disgusted at times that I would have to take self-imposed sabbaticals from any news source just to unwind. Nevertheless, I was able to cut through all the bullshit with nothing less than my uncommon common-sense. While conservative talk radio proved that millions of others felt as I did about what America ought to be, talk without action was becoming cheap.

What I wanted was fire and brimstone and few were willing or as compassionate as I in their philosophy. Since I could no longer expect the Republican Party to stand on principle, I figured I had to do something to set the record straight on what most Americans, at least those with common-sense were thinking, if not saying. I also wanted to prove that I could do something Hillary Clinton had failed to do in her first two books, that is, I would write my own book and I would tell the truth.

Unlike most political books that require years of research replete with scores of references that rival the length of the book itself, I would write this book from a pure common-sense perspective with mostly my memory to rely on. So, if I forget to reference some tidbit of information, it isn't because I'm lazy. Because I have a real job and a family, time for research is limited and money for staff is non-existent until I sell a million copies.

Now, unlike our lofty liberal friends, I'll admit I'm no scholar and I certainly wasn't born a genius, but what I do have is common-sense and apparently lots of it. Since I am also an American, I have the right to express my common-sense and, yes, you have the right not to read it. But, unlike the loony Left, I won't try to force my ideas on you. However, I will point out how stupid you are if you don't accept them as the way things ought to be. In fact, I have been blessed with so much common-sense that many of you may even consider me a prodigy of sorts after reading this book. You will certainly think twice before judging all Redneck Americans to be nothing more than a bunch of stupid yokels. You see, I have found that love of country and common-sense is as natural for most Rednecks as stupidity and anti-Americanism is for most liberals.

Because it takes years for the average idiot to develop his/ her stupidity, I realize that it may take many more years for the common-sense impaired to come to my level of understanding. After all, it wasn't until I was in my early twenties that I realized just how fortunate I was to have been blessed with an inordinate amount of common-sense. Believe me, I used to sit up at night and wonder what the Good Lord had given me that would allow me to succeed in life. There were, after all, the athletically and musically gifted, along with all those Trust-fund babies; surely He had reserved something for me.

I figure God must have sparked my interest in politics that fateful night just so I could realize my gift and bestow it upon you. I suppose also that all that common sense must have had something to do with the reality of my situation, which was a life created by and later devoted to self-reliance. Besides, growing up a latchkey kid in a single-parent household doesn't leave one with many choices. Having a Mom straight off the boat from Germany in 1966 didn't help much either. At least so I once thought.

Though she may not have been ready for the Redneck in-laws, life in America sure must have been preferential to what post-WWII Germany had to offer. While her prospects had been greatly improved by moving to the land of the free, I don't think she initially grasped the idea that in America, opportunity was always just around the corner. And while she may not have known that her choice of a husband and father would fall short of his duties, she did do her best as a stranger in a new land. Hell, as far as I'm concerned now, making it to America was the best thing she could have ever done for me.

By the age of nineteen, mom had already spent her first twelve years in worthless communist East Berlin and seven subsequent years in a not quite as worthless socialist West Berlin. All of which, I imagine, instilled in her certain beliefs that would take many years in America to dispel. One belief that I constantly tried to instill in her was that in America it was every parent's dream to give their children a better life than they had. Still, no matter how relevant my arguments were, all attempts at fostering better international relations usually fell on deaf ears. It was only later—when I compared her experience in Germany to mine in America—that I realized she did give me a better life than she had had.

I can still remember her response in heavily accented German, when I told her that I wanted to go to college: "Schteeven, college ist a place vere de rich send der childrens so dey don't havt to verk! Ven you graduate from de high schkool you get a full-time job!" At first, I thought this was just an excuse because she couldn't afford to send me to college. Now that I've spent many years working inside corporate America and along side many college graduates, I'm inclined to agree with her assessment.

Though it didn't always seem that way, growing up somewhat poor was actually a good thing for me, because that life offered me opportunities to learn things that I am now able to teach my own children. Lessons that originated out of circumstance, now afford me the opportunity to expand my own children's horizons. In addition, it has afforded me the opportunity to say with a straight face: "Stop your whining! Why, when I was a kid, I didn't have all the things you have and if I wanted something I had to work for it!"

No, I didn't get that go-cart I always wanted, but not getting it taught me that if I wanted something I would have to work for it. When I was nine years old, the thing that I wanted most was a go-cart, but I quickly realized I wasn't going to get one. So I decided to build my own. While it didn't have an engine, there were a few hills in the area and on occasion I even managed to sucker someone into pushing me around or allowing me to tie a rope to the back of their bike.

My first attempt at building a go-cart required only four items: lawn mower wheels, 2x4s, a piece of rope for steering, and about a half pound of 16-penny nails. Since most of my relatives were carpenters and I spent many a summer at various job sites working as a gofer, these items were readily available. Being a gofer meant that you were low man on the totem pole, since it was your job to "go for" this or "go for" that; hence, gofer. I know most of you probably didn't need an explanation, but I've no doubt that others would have been left scratching their heads and those on the Left were probably reaching for their phones to call and complain to someone about child labor laws.

The nails I used in building the go-cart not only helped to assemble the parts but also made not-so-great axles. The average lawnmower wheel required about eight 16-penny nails hammered into the end of a 2x4 to create an axle. The trick was to use just enough so that the wheel could rotate and still remain attached. To ensure that the nails were hammered in a circular manner, I used a dime as my guide to draw a circle at each end of the 2x4. One nail was all that was usually needed to create a pivot point for the front axle to swing from the front to the rear and allow steering. All that was left to do was to attach that 4-foot piece of rope at each end of the front axle and I was ready to roll.

This childhood experience gave me the idea to build for my first son—a Batman freak—his own soapbox Batmobile. Only this time I designed and built the go-cart with bolts and real axles, and it even included a center-mounted shock absorber at the front. But payback is hell, because I was the sucker who got to push and pull him around the neighborhood. Still, I must admit I beamed with pride when I pulled him and his dog to his first day of school. There wasn't a boy in sight who didn't look on in admiration of this wooden caricature of the Batmobile.

Not only did the experience of building my own go-cart help me to be self-reliant, it also taught me how to be innovative. From my first attempt at what was more a rickety soapbox cart than a go-cart to the experience of owning an MG (which I foolishly bought my senior year in high school), I learned a lot about how mechanical things work. My first car was a perfectly reliable 1976 Ford Pinto; the last year of the exploding model. Though the Pinto got me from point A to point B, it wasn't very cool. So I sold it for $400 and with the addition of another $400 that I had managed to save, I bought an MG. That piece of crap broke down the first day I got it home. I grew to hate that car, but it too, taught me a lot: 1) how cars are suppose to work, and 2) how British cars rarely work. After graduating from high school, I was driving another Pinto. Only this time, it was a 1980 model, and Ford had corrected the exploding problem in all '77 and later models.

Yes, I was poor, but I was a poor American, which meant I was still better off than 95% of the world's population. Being an American also meant that I didn't have to stay poor. My minimalist standard of living had made me self-reliant, and that taught me how to think, which helped me acquire the vast amounts of common sense that I can now bestow upon you. For example, it's not smart to pour a gallon of gasoline on a driveway and throw a match on it, even if your friend assures you that it will burn off in a matter of seconds. Luckily, Mom wasn't due home for hours and we were able to brush off most of the slightly charred areas of the house.

I also learned that plywood surfing in a pasture full of bull nettles (itchy weeds from hell) isn't very smart either. This stunt is accomplished by tying a strip of plywood to the back of any motorized vehicle. Plywood that is 3/8 of an inch thick is preferable, as it is more flexible. Bendable wood is a must in order to place a curve at the front of your board and avoid the other hazardous dangers found in a pasture: cow patties and salt licks.

Still, were it not for cousins that gave Rednecks a bad name, I wouldn't have spent a week peeing on my legs. This just happened to be, as my Grandfather assured me, the only way to stop the stinging caused by a bull nettle. As for the smell, well, it went away with a shower. And as for those cousins, let me just say revenge is sweet. You see, pasture surfing is so much fun everyone wants a turn.

While there was once a time in America when most people were sufficiently equipped with common-sense, I no longer believe that to be the case. I can only surmise that the use of common-sense in the past must have had more to do with American attitudes towards self-reliance than some innate force. This simple deduction of mine is based on nothing more than my observations of current-day America. What many Americans used to do for themselves they now pay others to do for them. Gone is that old adage, "Why pay someone to do for you what you can do for yourself?"

Though I never felt like being poor was much of a hindrance, it did leave me wanting in a few areas during my high school years. Even then I probably would not have cared had the affections of many a fox (80s lingo for hot chicks) not required that I be dressed in trendy clothes and have a cool car. Which I suppose, was the real reason for the MG. But I'm not whining about that and I don't think there should be a social program to buy trendy clothes or cool cars for poor kids. I never wanted to kill the rich kids or to blame others for my family's lack of cash and I don't recall my Mom ever standing in a government line for cheese, food stamps, or welfare either.

By the time I was nine years old, I realized that if I wanted something, I would either have to wait until Christmas, if it wasn't affordable, or I would have to push my lawn mower up and down the street and ask people if they wanted their lawn mowed. Besides, I had a bike, plenty of friends, and usually a couple of bucks in the back pocket of my tough-skins. What else did I really need? I was living the life of Theodore "Beaver" Cleaver even if I didn't have the quintessential father.

Because I lived what was once the stereotypical life of a boy in America, it's easy to compare and contrast my experiences with those of most boy's today. Granted, video games weren't nearly as sophisticated then as they are today, but even so, you would have rarely caught me inside playing videos, watching TV, or talking on the phone for hours like some kind of a nancy-boy. Just how is a boy to develop the skills necessary to guide him through life, if he spends his time inside separated from the real world? That many would rather stay inside today, is only further testament to the Left's success at emasculating many boys for the purpose of turning them into pacifistic dumbasses. From the anti-gender based social engineering schemes of the Left, to the doctors who prescribe psychotic drugs like candy; many boys are simply not having the experiences necessary to turn them into men.

I suppose also that some of the blame for this could be attributed to the many useless—I've never created a thing in my life—personal injury (PI) attorneys. One of my favorite pastimes as a boy used to be rummaging through junkyards. I can remember riding my bike with friends to a junkyard near my home. It was just across the street from a dirt track where my Dad used to race cars. My friends and I would search the floorboards and seat crevices of all those junk cars for any lost or forgotten change we could find. If we were lucky, we would scavenge enough to buy a pop for the five-mile ride back home. The owner never cared; he knew we were just boys being boys.

I also remember an old grain mill along the way that had concrete floors as slippery as an ice rink from the tons of grain that had smoothed its surface over the years. We would get to hauling ass, as fast as we could on our bikes and as soon as we hit that slippery surface, we would hit the brakes and lay our bikes over to see who could slide the furthest. Man, was that fun! Whose fault do you think it would have been if I had gotten hurt? Mine, of course, and whose fault would it be today? If you ask a PI attorney, I'm sure he'll tell you... "the owners of that old mill."

Because a bunch of dumbass plaintiffs and their jackass attorneys are determined to prove that nobody is responsible for themselves anymore, just about everything we do now is controlled by government, dictated by insurance companies or imposed on us by business and property owners. We're no longer allowed to step off the trail, to go here or there, or to do this or that without the permission or mandate of government or some poor guy worried about getting his ass sued off.

You know, I've been around the block a few times, I keep up with current events and I even read often of past events. And while I've traveled more than the average bear, I wouldn't profess to being one of the world's greatest traveler. Still, from these experiences I can say with the utmost of confidence that America is the best. Even at our worst, we are immensely better than the rest. We are truly the greatest country that has ever existed. There has never been any other like us, either past or present, and I suspect there will never be any in the future. I sometimes feel sorry for those on the Left, because they can't feel what so many real Americans do for their country and its accomplishments. Maybe that is why the Left hates America so much; they just don't have the emotional connection to, or the understanding of, what America is all about.

Though it makes me feel a little goofy to admit it, but to this day I find it difficult to listen to the National Anthem without getting glassy-eyed. I'm not sure why that is, but I think it may have something to do with all those WW II documentaries I watched on PBS as a kid. Even as a teenager I would stay up late into the evening when most stations were signing off just to hear the National Anthem played. During sign-off, there was one particular station—I can't remember which—that would play the National Anthem while an American flag waved in the foreground of majestic mountains. As added emphasis to this patriotic scene, an F-16 would roar by under clear blue skies at the very end. I'll tell you what, that scene alone use to give me the goose bumps. How anyone can witness that and not be moved, is beyond me.

Now, if that doesn't motivate you enough to want to learn more about, "Why Rednecks Will Save America Again" then hopefully your curiosity will. If so, I hope that when you have finished this book you will sit back and think about why America is so great, and why you should be doing everything possible to ensure that She stays that way.

Chapter 2

Losers

"A government that is big enough to give you all you want is big enough to take it away."   Barry Goldwater

At the risk of sounding like some crotchety old coot, I have got to tell you... I sure do miss the good old days. It's not that I object to today's modern conveniences, mind you; I just long for the days in America when patriotism and the right to exist for one's own self was not only unquestioned, but expected. Since I'm probably not the only one who would appreciate a return to the good old days—philosophically speaking of course—I'm almost certainly not the only one thinking it may just require another Revolution. I'm thinking we can even kick this one off Southern style too, our own "Boston Tea Party" of sorts. Only this time, instead of tea, we can dump truck loads of government cheese into the mouth of the Mississippi. Hell, we might even get a twofer out of this one. Government cheese has been backing-up millions of Americans for years; imagine what it might do to shore-up the levies in Louisiana.

If you're thinking that another Revolution might be too drastic, I am open to suggestions. But, I've got to tell you, I'm pretty set on the idea of a Revolution being the only viable way to take America back from the ruling elite and their hordes of political minions. Besides, it doesn't have to be a bloody one. I'm sure the mere sight of just a few hundred Rednecks taking up positions around San Fransissysco in 4x4s and swamp buggies would be enough to scare the entire city into submission. I don't know about you, but just thinking of an America where socialists and communists once again find it necessary to gather secretly in their hovels and speakeasies is enough to get me all giddy inside.

While the envy-ridden loser may no longer find it necessary to dwell in the underbelly of American society, I'm confident that it's nothing a little red-baiting couldn't handle. Hell, if we would just bring back the House Committee on un-American Activity most of these nut-jobs would fall right back into relative obscurity. Not even the envy-ridden loser would be foolhardy enough to take his ideas to the streets if he feared reprisal. Sure, dramatic events similar to the Great Depression or the Vietnam War might bring many of these loons out of their holes, but wouldn't most temper their anti-American sentiments if Americans stopped being so damn apathetic? Certainly the gathering of thousands of losers en masse to openly bash America and burn the flag could be minimized.

Should you believe that the crazies are too few in number to be concerned with, I ask you to think again. Today, the Left is solidly one-third of the American electorate. Know also that it was American indifference towards this lunatic fringe in the 1960s that they can now spread their anti-Americanism undeterred. No longer fearful of reprisals from true Americans, few leftists even make the effort to hide their true intentions and have no qualms with mocking traditional American values. For them, patriotism and nationalism is little more than an exhibition of white racism and greed.

With no real response likely from mainstream America, the Left's assault on all things traditionally American will probably continue for years and years to come. It would seem that middle-class living has so numbed the largesse that rendering an opinion on anything controversial is no longer possible. The Left, having proceeded for nearly five decades undeterred, has apparently convinced millions that personal responsibility and self-reliance are truly nothing more than right-wing speech for racism and selfishness.

In their zeal to reshape America as a socialist nation, they have even attempted and succeeded to some degree in rewriting our Nation's history. Just how, I will cover in Chapter 6. Still, what each new generation is now being taught is that America's achievements come not from individualism, the U.S. Military or the sacrifices of our Forefathers, but from collectivism, big government and multiculturalism. Not even the Founding Fathers, U.S. Military or Christianity itself is safe from these losers.

Though the Left and millions of unappreciative Americans may not accept it, it is an undeniable truth that every American owes a debt of gratitude to our Nation's Forefathers and to the men and women who have fought and now fight to preserve our Nation. While it is obvious that our military deserves the lion's share of gratitude for preserving our freedoms, recently I've been questioning just what it is that they are fighting to preserve. Whatever their reasons were for choosing to defend the country,

I'm relatively sure that few, if any, signed-up to preserve the ideas of a bunch of anti-American losers.

When I joined the Air Force, I swore to uphold the Constitution of the United States, not the United Nations Charter or any other document of a foreign nation. When I took the 'Oath of Allegiance' I meant it, and I expected others who took the oath to live and die by it too. So, why do you suppose it is, that millions of men and women in the military with high school diplomas can understand their oath, but others with far greater levels of education can't seem to grasp its meaning? While I'm asking the questions; why do you also suppose it is that "We the People" no longer expect those having taken the oath to live by it either?

Well, if we have no intention of holding someone to his or her word, then why bother? Is it really too much to ask of an American today, to stand by their word in matters of importance? I ask these questions not out of cynicism, but because past and present elected and appointed officials have and continue to thwart the Constitution without any fear of reprisal.

Just what is it that they stand to lose should they perform their duty? It isn't as though we've asked them to give their lives as appointed or elected officials. If you find my line of questioning to be reasonable, then you will most certainly understand why it is that I get pissed off when I hear an impeached President refer to the UN Charter as the greatest document ever written, or when I see US military personnel being forced to wear UN helmets and patches.

It's bad enough that most politicians no longer find it necessary to act on behalf of the Constitution that even some members of the highest court in the land feel embolden to regularly rule against it and usually in favor of some loser or group of losers.

The willingness of some US Supreme Court Justices to legislate from the bench and take decisions contrary to the express intent of the Constitution should be disconcerting to all Americans. If you need an example, you have only to read or listen to some of their more recent opinions.

For example, in a 2003 ruling on whether states have the right to criminalize sodomy, (Lawrence v Texas) Justice Kennedy gave as his reason for overturning anti-sodomy laws, the changing views of a "wider civilization." Don't get me wrong, I don't believe the courts belong in our bedrooms either, but by way of Justice Kennedy's reasoning, in matters of U.S. law, we are only to consider the viewpoint of a "wider civilization" and to hell with the Constitution. That's funny, because I always thought that Supreme Court decisions had to be based on the rule of law, not the collective views of a bunch of losers.

To show their appreciation for Kennedy's remarks, both Justices Breyer and O'Connor brought into question the vitality of a Constitution that is over two centuries old in a society that is increasingly global. Justice Ginsberg, never one to allow any doubt as to her bias, has gone so as far as to argue the "legitimacy of a document that conflicts with so many other documents of foreign nations." It would seem that by their estimation, the Constitution is a relic of the past and not in keeping with the times or at least their vision of a world community. If they had any integrity they would do us all a favor and admit to their true intentions and resign from their position. After all, if we have only to rely on the wisdom of world opinion, then what good are they?

Their way of thinking is exactly what our Forefathers had hoped to avoid. In fact, our Forefathers were so concerned about this that the Constitution we know today was not ratified until some 13 years after the Declaration of Independence. Why so long? Well, aside from fighting a Revolution, it seems that some states were not entirely comfortable with the initial drafts of the Constitution. Many of the Constitutional Delegates felt that the newly proposed Constitution of 1787 was ambiguous at best. Greater clarity with respect to powers granted to the federal government, the rights of individuals and those of the several States was demanded.

I might also add that those making such demands came primarily from the South. These Southerners would get their way when born out of their inherent distrust for the federal government; the "Bill of Rights" was created. This addendum, if you will, was meant to ensure that should any wide-eyed politician or bureaucrat get to feeling too good about himself, the people would be within their rights to remove him by whatever means necessary.

When most people think of the Constitution, it is the Bill of Rights that usually comes to mind. It is also the Bill of Rights, or the original Ten Amendments that has become the most recognized and debated portion of our Constitution. The original intent of the Bill of Rights was to simply clarify to all, including the federalists of the past and the leftists and neo-conservatives of today that certain rights are unalienable and are not to be tampered with. Unfortunately, in the many discussions I have had with people regarding the Constitution, I have found that very few even understand what an unalienable right is.

For those who have forgotten their high school civics lessons on the Constitution and for those who never got one, unalienable rights are those rights that can neither be granted nor taken away. They exist with or without government. What does this mean? It means that the Constitution—or more specifically the Bill of Rights—does not grant us our rights, as today's revisionists would have you believe. The Bill of Rights simply recognizes their inherent existence. To put it yet another way, you are born with them. If an analogy will help, inherent rights are to humans what instincts are to animals, they simply exist upon birth.

For those incapable of seeing the obvious until it smacks them in the face; the American Constitution exists for the express purpose of limiting the power of government and promoting the free will of men. It protects only the rights of the individual, as unalienable rights are wholly related to the individual and not to any particular collective (group) or entity. The beauty of our Constitution is the simplicity in which it was written and how those words are as applicable today as they were over 200 years ago. The Constitution is not a living and breathing document subject to change every time a bunch of losers want to force their ideas down the throats of true Americans.

Unlike the tyrannical monarchies of their day, America's Forefathers fully understood that no government should ever be entrusted with the power to grant or exclude unalienable (inherent) rights. Because they understood the corrupting affect of absolute power, they put in place three branches of government; the Executive, Judicial and Legislative to operate as a system of checks and balances. Among other things, these three branches were meant to act as safeguards for the protection of each and every American's unalienable rights. The only flaw in their design that I have been able to identify is that they made no provisions for guaranteeing the future character of men.

Read enough American history and study the Constitution long enough and you'll soon realize that our Forefathers were only recognizing the natural state of man's existence, that is, a man's right to exist and act on his own behalf. Of course, this does not mean that we can do entirely as we wish. In a civil society, it simply means that government has no authority to control us within our fundamental (natural) rights. But, because we have free will there is no guarantee that men will always act justly and for this reason we are also a nation of laws. While laws of any sort are enforced by government created (unnatural) entities, all such entities must act in the interests of an individual's (natural) rights.

If the Constitution were to recognize any entity or collective as having rights, then our system of government would be prejudicial towards the individual. For example, among the many rights recognized by our Constitution, is the individual's right to petition the government for a redress of grievances. What this means, is that individuals are entitled to a remedy for legitimate complaint. If collective desires took precedence over individual rights then there might never be a legitimate complaint. All that would be needed to make illegitimate, an individual's complaint, would be for two or more people to form a collective and protest on its behalf. Had this been allowed by our Constitution, the individual would almost always have found himself at the mercy of any mob, collective or entity of the government.

Unfortunately, we don't have to think too long and hard to find examples of where the federal government has rendered the 1st Amendment and others useless. If you're at a loss, I offer the nonsense of Affirmative Action and the stupidity of "Hate Crimes" legislation as examples enough to prove my point. In either case, the federal government has chosen to put aside individual rights in favor of groups defined as having a disadvantage. If, according to the "Equal Rights Act" it is against the law to discriminate against an individual based on their race, religion, sex or national origin, and soon their sexual orientation, then why is it not against the law to discriminate in favor of an individual belonging to a particular race, religion or lifestyle?

No other nation in the history of mankind, either past or present, has ever recognized the distinct rights of the individual as enumerated in the American Constitution. As a matter of fact, so new was the concept that initially many Americans found the idea of individual rights to be an absurd abstraction. Individual liberty was so foreign a concept that even the oppressed openly ridiculed it. Based on newspaper articles and private letters of the time it has been estimated that initially, less than a third of all Americans even supported the Revolution. Though, if truth be told, their lack of support for the Revolution probably had more to do with a desire to maintain personal security than a desire to secure liberty. It seems that for some, servitude over freedom for the sake of security was best and that renouncing the King would be better left to the more adventurous.

Well, it seems that the more things change the more they stay the same, as history appears to be repeating itself. No, I'm not worried about England reestablishing the monarchy and reclaiming US territories. However, I am concerned that like some pre-Revolutionary War Americans, Americans today are all too willing to sacrifice their freedom for supposed security. According to every survey or poll conducted with respect to social programs, fewer than half of all Americans support abolishing all or some entitlement (welfare) programs including social security. Of course, the use of "entitlement" is a gross misuse of the word, because by my estimation, approximately 90% of the people receiving such benefits are not entitled to all or part of them.

To be entitled to something, one must either own or earn it. I still have enough common-sense to know that sitting on one's ass entitles you to nothing, including; an education, a job, money, food, clothing, transportation or a home. If you need to know anything about your government know that entitlements exist only as a means of empowering the State. Given America's most humble beginnings and past attitudes towards self-reliance, you would think that entitlements like welfare wouldn't even be possible. After all, America is a nation built mostly by individuals adhering to the idea of self-reliance and not by a bunch of envy-ridden losers.

If you do not agree that most politicians are selling out the country in exchange for power, then I ask you to simply observe the next election cycle. Watch the news, listen to the pollsters or ask a group of voters yourself... why they are voting for particular candidates? What you are likely to hear, is that a candidate was chosen for what he promised to give to them or their particular group. Yes, it is a sickening prospect, especially when you consider that few will ever realize that they are sanctioning the confiscation of property with each vote they cast for their favorite political pimp.

Now, if it were their wealth being exchanged for the so-called risk-free life, I wouldn't give a rat's ass, but their socialist utopia is costing me and others a boat-load of money, not to mention infringing on my right to life, liberty, and the pursuit of happiness. I'm not sure about you, but it doesn't make me particularly happy to see a bunch of losers living off the wealth I and others created. To make matters worse, the productive class has to suffer the persistent claims by liberal and neo-con politicians alike that they are the very reason for the plight of the loser.

Now, I can understand why the creators and perpetrators of the mob do what they do, they are simply envious, power hungry and/or vindictive fools. They are who they are and I realize that you can't change the majority of them, but what about the rest of America? Do they have to give-in or compromise their beliefs just to get along? If you are one who has chosen to remain silent for fear of riling a bunch of politically correct dumbasses, you should know that all you are doing is accepting their position and philosophically just as much a loser. Remember also that once the socialists have gained the majority of power, the ability to create wealth will belong almost exclusively to the politicians and their corrupt minions.

You have only to consider the following definition of socialism, to see my point: Socialism as an economic system provides for the State a scheme by which the means of production, the level of services, and the methods by which they are delivered can be controlled. Does Congress and bureaucracies like the EPA not strive to control the use of private land and natural resources? Does the State not provide specific services to government sanctioned groups at the expense of others? Do all socialists not want to control the method by which certain services (i.e., medical care) are delivered? Answer these few questions, and you'll see why it is that the only people who support the communal life or desire a socialist State are life's losers and those who wish to rule over them.

Chapter 3
The "ist" Factor

*"Democracy extends the sphere of individual freedom,
socialism restricts it. Democracy attaches all possible value
to each man; socialism makes each man a mere agent, a
mere number. Democracy and socialism have nothing in
common but one word: equality. But notice the difference:
while democracy seeks equality in liberty, socialism seeks
equality in restraint and servitude." Alexis de Tocqueville*

N ow that you have some idea of just who the losers are in
America, you need only to consider who it is that benefits
most from their collective stupidity to understand why it is that
they have any influence at all. While almost all government
agencies and bureaucracies benefit from serving the collective
desires of losers; the primary beneficiary is usually the politician,
i.e., the political pimp, labeled as such, for his ability to not
only profit from the work and misery of others, but to screw as
many innocent people in the process. Throw in a like-minded

liberal press and you have all the components necessary for the propagandizing of false grievances and the subsequent taking of liberty and property from the productive.

Thanks to the relentless whining of a bunch of losers about things others have supposedly done to make their irresponsible lives seem meaningless, productive and responsible Americans are being robbed daily of their wealth and liberty. In what can only be described as living in some sort of bizarre parallel universe at times, these thieves of liberty and wealth have the sheer audacity to portray themselves as liberators and the productive as the oppressors. Call me stupid, but I always thought that being forced to do something against your will was the true definition of oppression.

Despite all the Left's whining and crying about inequality, don't think for a second that it has anything to do with gaining equality. Though most with common-sense and regular bathing habits are acutely aware of this; others through either neglect or acceptance, have allowed the un-bathed, unthinking and unaccomplished to force their will upon them. The American character that I have come to know and respect never endeared itself to the incessant whining of the lazy and stupid. After all, why would we want to emulate the French, and since when does rejection equal oppression anyway?

If I were to use liberal logic (an oxymoron), then there are a lot of women out there guilty of oppressing me. Should I therefore have the right to demand satisfaction from them? Since there is no constitutional right to being accepted by others—contrary to Bill Clinton's desires—I wouldn't think so. Certainly the Left can accept an individual's right to freedom of association. Isn't this why they hated the late Senator Joseph McCarthy? Were they not incensed when Senator McCarthy exposed their fellow communists and co-conspirators in the halls of government and Hollywood? Are they not the ones who cry "McCarthyism" when their so-called progressive, otherwise socialist or communist ideas are exposed?

While no loser is apt to agree that his socialist desires are driven by an out of control envy for the accomplished, all losers are in agreement that if you can't force equality on the front-end socially, then you do it on the back-end economically. This way they can at least guaranty an equality of results, if not an equality of ability. One does not have to be a conspiratorial nut to see that the goals and desires of losers are real; as both can be found pointedly stated in the many books, papers, internet sites, pamphlets, banners and placards found in bookstores, at libraries, on internet blogs and of course, at their protests and rallies. Though amazingly open in such venues—where the average citizen pays them little attention—they are often quick to retreat when enough Americans become aware of their intentions. It is only then that their talking heads will even attempt to cover-up the true intent of their social and economic agendas.

Leftist politicians understand fully that should any part of their agenda be exposed for what it is, true Americans will reject it and throw them out of office, at least in those parts of the country where the crazies haven't taken over. They are acutely aware of the fact that the frog must be boiled slowly if they are to be successful. Isn't this exactly why John Dean lost his party's nomination for President? He, unlike other leftist leaders, wasted little time in turning up the heat; leaving no question as to what his intentions were.

Whether threatened by the truth or when exposure is imminent, the Left can almost always be counted on to take the low road. One of their favorite tactics at defusing probable adversaries is the ad hominem attack. In hopes of re-directing attention elsewhere, conservatives can always count on being labeled a McCarthyite, Right-wing extremist or even a Nazi.

Joseph McCarthy, the U.S. Senator from Wisconsin (1947-1957) and the man for which "McCarthyism" was coined, was one of America's greatest commie hunters until his death in 1957. While nothing ever came of his accusations that communists in the State Department were working against American interests—only because they were given the "whitewash" by a Democrat controlled Senate—he is to this day so despised by the Left that they're still trying to re-write the history surrounding his efforts. When ad-hominem attacks aren't enough to send their opponents running; accusations of corruption, lack of fairness and even foul play can be expected.

As masters of propaganda, the truth without question is of little consequence to the Left. When threatened with exposure they can only hope that the public will forget, grow weary or simply move on. While many are overt in their tactics, others prefer a more subtle approach. Just how subtle will generally depend on the size of their constituency or the region of the Nation from which they operate. For instance, in the South, leftist politicians will often tone down their rhetoric so as not to offend regional customs and traditions. Although you would be hard pressed to find an honest liberal willing to admit to any of these tactics, I challenge anyone to prove me wrong.

Another manner in which they have attempted to manipulate the general public, has been to simply repackage whatever it is they're trying to sell. Yes, it's still the same old crap, but now it has a new label. By relabeling past programs and existing ideas, liberals–for the purpose of misinforming those who cannot think for themselves–have created a new lexicon in an attempt to gain their acceptance.

For instance, programs and ideas like welfare and socialism have become so despised by many Americans—because of the images they engender—that the Left now refers to each as either "entitlements" or "progressive economics" respectively. Although my personal favorite has got to be listening to one of these yahoos explain how income taxes are now "investments" in our future. You had better get your tissue ready, because these aren't just any old investments either; they are investments to ensure our children's future.

The truth is, that these so-called investments are meant only to ensure two things: 1) the future of Big Government, and 2) the jobs of the collective scum who will run it. The Left has become so consumed by their desire for power and dominance that I don't even think that it is possible for them to tell the truth, much less respect the general wishes of the American people. It seems that in this regard they are no different from their communist ratfink predecessors of the early 20th century.

Joseph McCarthy may have been overzealous to some and certainly politically motivated to others, but that doesn't change the fact that he and his committee rooted out several communists and American traitors in positions of power and influence stemming all the way back to the Franklin D. Roosevelt era. So, they can call me what they wish, because I don't give a damn. If you feel it's your right to control my life through economic and/or social schemes you are a scum-sucking commie dirt-bag and I wish Joseph McCarthy and his committee were here today to root your sorry ass out.

Still, one should be careful not to give too much credit to the average loser; he is a mere follower incapable of thinking for himself. Lacking any real ability to think objectively, the average loser can only react as he has been trained to. In fact, the average loser's opinions are usually learned in one or more of the following ways: 1) from the collective with which he associates, 2) from the many elitists (liberal idiots) that teach at America's universities and colleges, or 3) from the dominant liberal mainstream media. These methods of learning are, of course, in stark contrast to the traditional methods of learning chosen by those who possess the ability to think objectively and for themselves.

With an ever growing class of losers, no collective mob is ever short of finding new recruits. Like flies to stink, they are attracted to any collective willing to hear their complaint and offer them an excuse for whatever it is that haunts their fragile psyche. Were it not for the creation of collectives representing the desires of vengeful losers, most of these misguided nut-jobs would exist only in their isolated and estranged worlds.

Though collectives exist for many reasons, there is one shared message that can be heard emanating from most of them and that is that capitalism is the sole cause for their plight. Such claims by the Left only serve to prove my point further, as true laissez faire capitalism (free enterprise) seeks to rule over no one. Capitalism is a disinterested economic force where success is measured only by one's ability. In stark contrast, the success of socialism can only be measured by the amount of control the State can impose on individuals.

While most collectives are created to serve special interests or to unify enough losers around a particular goal or contrived plight, most have also been taken in by the Democratic Party to serve the larger goals of the Left's agenda. Alliances have been made much like those of the many socialist factions existing in every European country today. As these collectives (mobs of malcontents) were absorbed into the larger collective of the Democratic Party, the plight that once brought them together became secondary to the larger goal of destroying a capitalist and individualist America.

Despite their claims of oppression, these losers should never be seen as anything more than an ever-growing class of self-repressed individuals joined together by an out of control envy of the successful. Besides, only a collective mob of idiots could make the claim that as long as we eat meat, we are sanctioning the murder of animals or that if we continue to build new homes and drive SUVs we will destroy the planet and that if we defend ourselves against some evil despot of color, we are racists. All I can say is, 'Thank God, Hitler was white.' Had he been a fascist of color we might never have won WWII. Think I'm wrong again, then check out what's going on in Darfur or what the dictator Mugabe has done to Zimbabwe.

Up until now I've portrayed losers in the broadest of terms by referring to them as: socialists, leftists, liberals and communists. But, just who exactly are they? Well, they are; marxists, anarchists, unionists, altruists, extreme environmentalists, abortionists, multiculturalists, ethnocentrists, feminists, terrorists, animal-rights activists, gay-rights activists and any other "ist" with a bitch about something that someone else has supposedly done to make their self-loathing, irresponsible, immoral lives seem meaningless.

Somehow, these freakazoids have gotten it into their heads that they cannot exist without the wealth and approval of the very people they hate. You see, without your apathy and money they have no power, as their laziness makes existence very difficult. You say, "But Steve, I've never given these losers any money, how could I have empowered them?" Unfortunately, this is where many Americans stop thinking. They never stop to ask, "What the hell is going on here, and where have all my tax dollars been going, and why are these freaks influencing American policy?"

You see, just because some loser hasn't personally accosted you on the street for the money in your back pocket, it doesn't mean that he's not getting it in some other way.

Odds are, if you work, you are taxed, and those taxes are disbursed in the form of transfer payments. These payments are sent to government-sponsored groups, otherwise known as voting blocs (collective mobs). For those of you who still don't get it, politicians (political pimps) are using your money to buy the votes of losers to keep them in power. The system is mutually inclusive as it benefits both the political pimp and the collective mob. By working together, the political pimp can have his lust for power satisfied, and the collective mob (his whores) can have their overwhelming feelings of envy assuaged. But like a drug addict, the satisfaction fades quickly with each successive dose, and it isn't long before the collective is seeking its next fix, that is, more of your money and acceptance.

To this day, the expansion in the number of losers continues, as those once straddling the fence between independence and dependence fall further and further to the left with each promise of a new handout. It seems that the draw of the collective is just too powerful for some to resist, as many will take their last free choice as an individual and choose to exist only for the benefit of others. Sadly, most will never even realize that they were only being used as a means to another's end.

Without any serious challenge coming from real Americans, losers will only continue to amass in size. It is truly up to real Americans everywhere to decide whether or not they will remain apathetic or fight for their liberty. If speaking-up isn't your thing, then at least show up at the ballot box. If for no other reason, just to send a message to politicians that it is not in their interest to sell out America for the sake of personal wealth and power. Because if we fail now, there may be no alternative in the future.

As always, it is the apathetic American who is the unwitting ally in the assault on American culture. If apathetic Americans would just become engaged in the debate or at a minimum, judgmental of those seeking to destroy the economic and moral framework of America; then perhaps the anti-American Left in all its forms and collectives, could be relegated back to the fringes of society.

Not even an amoral politician would bother listening to a bunch of disaffected losers if there was nothing to be gained. Hell, if held accountable for their actions, some might even take their "Oath of Office" seriously. But, I suppose we shouldn't expect too much from someone who would sell their soul for the power it might bring. You may think that such people could never have full control of America, but I have to ask, why should they have any control of America? What do you suppose will happen when the losers outnumber the producers and mob rule is imposed? I'll tell you what will happen, it will mean the destruction of the family and America as it was intended.

The only reason why I, and many others recognize what is going on is that we care enough to pay attention. The problem is that for every one of us who do care, there are just as many, if not more, which do not. Unfortunately, I don't know how to make apathetic Americans care before they realize that they have been duped. Perhaps if they understood the process and could recognize when they were being manipulated they would care. For those of you who do not understand the process and who are willing to make an effort, I'll attempt an explanation.

The Explanation:

America's Democrats engage in a process I like to refer to as "political incrementalism." Political incrementalism is a process of pushing an agenda to gain as much ground as possible before maximum resistance is met, only to pull back when a new norm has been realized. Only when a new relative norm has been accepted, will there be an attempt to push the boundaries even further. For the leftist, the most opportune time to do so is during economic, cultural, or international unrest. If the agenda is pushed too hard, the political pimp and his malcontents run the risk of losing an election by angering the mainstream. As noted earlier, when a backlash occurs and the Left has realized that public opinion is against them, they will often retreat to the middle by espousing moderate, and in extreme cases, even conservative points of view.

An example of a hard push would be Bill Clinton's attempt to make homosexuality an acceptable standard for the military or even Hillary's first attempt to force socialized medicine (Hillary-Care) down our throats. Each push, bold in its own respect, was even bolder, if you consider that both were attempted in the first year of Bill's scandal-ridden presidency. I suppose we could thank them to some extent, as it was these and other actions that brought the Republicans to power in both houses of Congress in 1994. Unfortunately, it was little more than a wet dream for those of us who thought Republicans would be better. We didn't even have to wait for the next election cycle before they started breaking their promises on things such as term-limits.

There is hardly a demographic of our society that most politicians won't exploit to their advantage if it would help them gain control over the responsible. Gaining control over the irresponsible is easy enough, especially when you consider how easy losers succumb to handouts. But to do so over the responsible... well that usually requires methods that are most likely to tug at their heart strings. Just ask yourself, when was the last time you heard a politician tell you a new government program was needed because 94.4 percent of the population is working or that the average life expectancy is only 80 years of age? No, they are more apt to exploit the child of irresponsible parents or the elderly person who never planned for the future or even the illiterate adult who dropped out of school and never sought to better himself.

Though Hillary and her buffoon of a husband were never successful at implementing a socialized healthcare system, Republicans under the guidance of George W. Bush and his neo-conservative (neo-con) disciples would. By implementing the "Prescription Drug" benefit for the elderly, Bush and company effectively stole the issue from the Democrats. While "W" has been no friend of the Constitution, even I was admittedly taken aback when I learned that he had and continues to lobby Congress to approve a bill which would give social security benefits to illegal aliens. Apparently, it doesn't matter that they are here illegally, or that they benefited from numerous other government programs they never paid into. Ah, but what the hell, I suppose if you can't guarantee that it will be there for your own citizens, you might as well offer it to the world.

You would think that the creation of an entirely new bureaucracy would have been enough to placate their appetite for power, but it wasn't. It seems that "W" was just warming up when he took it upon himself in 2003 to give $15 billion of borrowed money to a bunch of savages in Africa more concerned with hacking-up their political rivals than distributing condoms. We hadn't even begun to touch the principal on this loan when in 2008 "W" promised another $48 billion. The initial $15 billion may have been intended to buy condoms to minimize the spreading of the AIDS virus, but most of it ended up in the foreign accounts of the ruling class. Apparently no one at the State Department bothered to mention to "W" that manliness in sub-Sahara Africa is measured by the amount of children sired. If we have to teach them something, why can't we teach them that a man is defined by how many children he can feed, not sire?

The boys and girls at the State Dept. might have also mentioned that tribal Africans already had a couple of ways of dealing with the virus anyway. I can't understand how a nation as technologically advanced as we are, could have missed this one either. The answer was right there all along. It seems that all one has to do to rid himself of the AIDS virus is to rape a virgin. And, apparently it doesn't matter the age either. For the savage not taken to such brutality, all is not lost. As practitioners of the ancient art of sub-Saharan voodoo, many also believe that an incantation performed by an African witch doctor will also rid them of the disease.

Now, if I was able to learn of these human tragedies by simply watching a documentary on PBS, why wasn't the President made aware of it? And if he was, why did he still give them $63 billion of money we had to borrow from the Chinese? Just what in the hell is the State Department telling this dumbass? Have they not been attending their own diversity training classes? If "W" and his administration really want to save these people, they'll need to find the sane among them and give them weapons.

Even though Republicans have co-opted a portion of the Left's platform and continue to compromise their own positions, they are still many years behind the Left's ability to brainwash the weak. Learned from their communist and fascist brethren of years past, they understood early on the value of brainwashing at an early age. Even when their preferred method of persuasion fails or access to our youth is denied, they are rarely short of finding victims. Or should I say, creating them? It is no coincidence that the mentally weak make up a majority of the Democratic Party , as they are most willing to accept themselves as being victims of some mythical oppressive white state.

The goal of creating a mythical enemy for the disaffected has been a tactic employed by the power hungry for centuries. Hitler used communists and Jews as his scapegoats, Stalin would use Capitalists and the Jews as his, and radical Islam—not to be outdone by either—would use and continue to use the Jews, Capitalists, and all of Western culture as theirs. Since the Left's world is one of relativism and perception, an enemy is a must in order that the weak-minded might be persuaded to follow. You see, for the leftist, it is all about feelings or more accurately, the perception of feelings, no matter how idiotic the claim.

When backed into a corner and forced to debate an actual issue, the leftist will often resort to ad hominem (name calling) attacks, as reason and logic are non-existent in his argument. Tell me, what conservative hasn't been charged with insensitivity, of being uncaring, or full of hate because they refuse to go along with the Left's socialist schemes. The self-anointed champions of the 1st Amendment may demand that all have a right to speak and be heard, but they're the first to shun it by way of political correctness when it threatens to expose them for who they are.

I have no doubt in my mind that the philosophical and political beliefs of these people stem from a mental deficiency, whether induced by envy or a maniacal nature. Why else would someone insist on destroying something proven to have benefited so many? Proponents of political correctness may vary in their degree of stupidity and evil, but one thing I am certain of is that these people are hell-bent on pushing their agenda and controlling some or all aspects of our lives. Whether it is teaching your kids that homosexuality is a good thing, telling you what you can eat or drive, banning cigarettes, rationing healthcare, confiscating private property, or extorting more of your money, they want to control your life to their benefit.

For leftists, collectivists, socialists, communists, and other "ists," it does not matter what you think if you are one of the two "ists" that has not been accepted by the "ist" culture—a capitalist and individualist. The capitalist or the individualist must be shunned by the Left, as the primary tenet of their philosophy is personal responsibility. The mere mention of responsibility for oneself will generally throw liberals into a catatonic fit, a fit usually filled with outlandish charges of cruelty being perpetrated on the people. All for the sheer audacity of expecting people to accept responsibility for their actions.

One has only to look at where liberals stand on the major issues of the day to find examples of their irresponsibility. For example, should one become homeless, unemployed, pregnant or addicted to drugs, it is never attributed to the individual's immoral actions. For the liberal, no individual is to be held morally accountable, especially when they have been empowered to make the malcontent whole at the expense of others. To add insult to extortion, there will be no time constraint placed on the individual to be made whole either. A liberal's work must be done no matter how long it takes or how much it costs someone else.

If I'm to accept their claim that no one has a right to impose his or her moral values on another, then why should I be forced to bear the expense? If you tell me that I am obligated to support those who will not support themselves, is that not still a moral position? Somehow they are capable of finding a Constitutional right to the confiscation of wealth, but can't recognize an individual's right to their own life, liberty and property.

If you would like a good laugh, just ask one of your local dumbasses to show you where in the Constitution it gives them the right to make productive citizens the slaves of the non-working. When they give you the usual simpleton response that no one is making anyone the slave of another, you should then ask them to define slavery. If they're honest, they'll tell you its forcing someone to do something against their will for the economic benefit of another. Well then, if a person is forced to pay taxes that are used to provide food, housing, and healthcare to others—others who will never bear any of its costs—just who is the economic beneficiary and who is the slave?

Don't kid yourself, when the average American works till mid-May just to pay his taxes, who do you think he is serving? According to the IRS, the top 50% of all wage earners in the United States pay 97% of all taxes. So, why aren't the recipients of all this coerced goodwill thankful? One would expect that such a sacrifice made by the productive citizens of America would warrant at least a thank you. To this day, I have yet to receive a single "Thank you" from the government or the recipients of all my coerced goodwill. Instead, I receive nothing but disdain, hatred and demands for more of what I've earned. Yeah, yeah, yeah... I know, it was probably years of oppression that made them that way. But hey, they shouldn't worry, because they're just an election cycle away from stealing more of what the top 50% earned.

It is pure and simple folks. Responsibility is all that life requires. While some of us will choose to accept it, others will not. You should be asking yourself, 'Why should I have to pay for those who will not?' Now, before I am judged as evil incarnate, I do make the distinction between those who are capable of accepting responsibility and those who are not. I am willing to take the moral position, along with others I hope, that those who truly cannot help themselves should be helped. But we should never let those in want of power decide who the incapable are. It should be self-evident as to which people are incapable of helping themselves. If you are incapable of using your common-sense to make this distinction, then you are an idiot.

To find further fault with the "ist" culture, we needn't look any further than the Communist Manifesto, which states, "To each according to his needs, from each according to his ability." For those of you who do not understand Marxist logic, it means; "You work for the benefit of others, not yourself." As with most Americans, I work primarily to provide food, shelter and clothing for my family. I don't have the time or the inclination to support the irresponsible, especially under government duress. So, does this make me, or anyone else, for that matter, cruel, rich, and evil? No! Do I seek to oppress the impoverished? Still no! Like many Americans, I've simply chosen to accept my responsibility in life.

Regardless of how the Left views the role of government in our lives, it is simply ridiculous to believe that they know better than us how to run our lives or that if we would just relent, utopia could be achieved. It's as though in their wacko world, the janitor is somehow of equal economic value to the doctor, or that the auto mechanic is of equal value to the busboy. Here are five questions you might ask one of your local dumbasses to answer when they start running-off at the mouth about economic equality:

1. How will you guarantee that each person will work as hard as the next?
2. What measures will be taken to guarantee that no man shall have abilities superior to another?
3. If everyone is equal from birth till death in all aspects of life, how then will progress be made?

4. What exactly is your vision of a perfect world, and how would you go about achieving it?
5. What will you do if someone refuses to accept your utopian views?

Because the Left cannot answer such questions truthfully without exposing their true intent, you shouldn't expect a thoughtful or logical answer. Having also been caught off-guard by an individual asking logical questions, the liberal will be quick to realize that he has been exposed for the dumbass that he is. Of course, this will be too much for him to bear and you will generally get one of two possible responses: 1) he will either attack you with one or more words from his mantra (Nazi, Racist, Homophobe, Eco-terrorist, Hate Monger, etc.) or 2) he will look at you like a deer caught in headlights with no way out.

Though it can be perplexing at times as to why so many are proponents of a system known to oppress and repress the inherent nature of man, you should never forget that for those at the top it has nothing to do with altruism and everything to do with power. The fact that socialism has failed in all its variants, means little to its followers either. Just know that the mind of a liberal must truly be a troubled one that they would burden so many others with such a disastrous system. We would all be wise to shun those so envious that they would readily demoralize a nation to assuage their feelings of inadequacy.

As for the leaders of any socialist movement, I understand that they are motivated by power and driven by their elitist belief that the common man is incapable of taking a decision that will affect his life. They certainly realize that once personal responsibility is taken from individuals, the state will be free to do as it wishes. Ultimately, if successful, the elite on both sides of the aisle will surely rejoice in capitalism's downfall, as we will become nothing more than the lab rats they wish us to be, caught up in their maze of social and economic schemes. We would all be wise to remember that a man who grows his own food has no need of a master, and believe me, we sure as hell don't need another five year plan to figure it out; we just need to be left alone.

I believe Benjamin Franklin summed it up best when he wrote:

"They that can give up essential liberty to obtain a little temporary safety deserve neither liberty nor safety."

Chapter 4

The So-Called Independent

"All that is necessary for evil to succeed is for good men to do nothing." Edmund Burke

While I have had an appreciation and respect for America's political, cultural and philosophical traditions for as long as I can remember, understanding why others didn't love America the way I do, has always been somewhat puzzling to me. For a while, I use to think as others still do that it was mostly the fault of the mainstream media or even that crap that's passed off as music today. But, as I always do, I got to thinking. Now, I'm inclined to think that it might be more accurate to say that the mainstream media is as much a victim of a concerted global effort to dumb down the world as are the rest of us.

Since the first time I heard George H.W. Bush utter the phrase "New World Order" I've been skeptical and uneasy about our government's intentions. After the more recent debates on immigration, education, the War and the selling off of American assets and corporations; the elitists, globalists and leftists have left me with no doubt as to what those intentions are and who their allegiances are with. They certainly don't seem to care in the least, what we the people think.

The stance taken by our so-called leaders on these issues must have gotten to a lot of people, as the gulf between both extremes of the two dominant parties widened even further. While approximately two-thirds of the population was busy fighting it out, others grew weary of the debates and disengaged all together. It would seem that for them, the prospect of thinking an issue out, coming to a conclusion and defending it would be all too taxing. As more and more became disinterested even the Press took notice. Though once the Press began to ask why, they took what was nothing more than a lazy and indifferent attitude on the part of many Americans and mislabeled them as Independents.

Should you be an Independent in the traditional sense, that is, you have an opinion but have chosen not to affiliate with any particular Party, this isn't meant as a criticism of you. What I'm referring to is the Independent, who rather than spare us his cowardice by taking the Fifth, extols the open-mind and willingness to compromise as virtues. Though the real truth is, he either has no opinion or is too afraid to give it.

For most Independents, the claim of being open-minded to an issue, is merely an attempt to defuse a situation. What this usually means, is that the Independent is in no better a position to render a coherent thought than is his lesser counterpart on the Left. Whether persuaded by populist whims or peer pressure, the Independent has chosen to have others do the thinking for him. Claims of independence to the contrary, the fear of not being accepted is enough to convince him that opposition among friends is better left to those more comfortable living a solitary life.

As you can now see, it's not just the Left causing America to sink further into a collective cesspool of stupidity and cowardice. As though the utter nonsense posed by the Left were not enough for right-thinking individuals to contend with, we also have to suffer at the hands of the flakey. The flakey may prefer that we refer to them as Independents, but since when does being an undecided fence-straddling suck-up make you independent of anything? Believe me, you don't have to spend much time around the so-called Independent to realize there is little depth to anyone who is more likely to compromise than stand on principle.

Though much smaller in number than the two dominant parties, Independent voters have garnered much attention in the last few Presidential campaigns. This is of course, only because they are large enough in numbers to swing an election in either direction. Though they have achieved recognition without effort, it has been their indecisive nature and wishy-washy stance on important issues that has exacerbated many of the problems we continue to face in our country. While hardcore ideologues are almost evenly divided on the Left and Right, the Independent voter is much more easily swayed. And, like a house full of whores on a Sunday morning, the politically ambitious know the easily swayed are out there; they're just looking for the next best way to suck them in.

Since many Independents simply lack thoughts sufficient enough to form opinions, the claim of being open-minded is a mere copout. The claim is also intended to shield an individual from criticism. Whether an opinion is right or wrong doesn't matter, what matters is how they are perceived. How else could one vote a mixed ticket or for a Republican one election cycle and yet a Democrat the next?

Does the Independent really not know that Liberals, if elected, will seek to raise taxes under the auspices of caring for the poor? Or that a true-Conservative, if elected, will most often try to lower taxes when not fearful of Democrat charges of insensitivity? Does he really believe that Conservatives represent only the rich and that Liberals truly feel for the poor? And, if so, why vote one way in an election cycle and yet another way in the next? How can they be for taxes, big government and abortion one year only to vote against them later?

If I have learned anything about the Independent, it is that the ideological or principled person is typically a turn-off to them, as they are unable to grasp the fact that with most of life's issues, things really are black and white. Instead, the Independent has chosen a life of confusion, having failed to grasp that a life lived in the middle is rarely right and is functionally wrong. Independents can hope to accomplish nothing when they try to replace fact-based reality with moral relativism.

Given their down-the-middle approach, the only thing I have found consistent about independent voters is that their convictions or lack thereof are inconsistent. This inconsistency is often expressed in much the same manner as the Left, that is, they have difficulty accepting particular certainties or believing that there is a right and a wrong side to a particular issue. Furthermore, their notion that peace and harmony can be achieved, if conflicting parties agree to a compromise, is an abandonment of all reason. If logic, reason and fact cannot change their minds, then maybe a review of unrevised history can.

The world is fraught with examples of compromise gone awry. Britain and France's compromise with Hitler gave us World War II. President Truman's compromise with China gave us present day North Korea. Bush #1 having compromised with Arab states following Gulf War I gave us 12 more years of Saddam Hussein, only to have his idiot son, Bush #2 mismanage an unnecessary Gulf War II. Also, let's not also forget that every idiot Democrat President elected since Truman has insisted on Israel compromising with a bunch of bloodthirsty Islamic freakazoids. These are just some of the compromises that caused the deaths of millions of innocent people.

What the Independent can't see is that before a compromise can be reached, both parties must have something to offer. What exactly is it that the Left has to offer? If their only offer is that I won't be arrested if I comply with their desires, then how can that be a compromise? Can we really expect bureaucrats and power hungry politicians to remember their place? While I'm asking the questions, can I ever expect a welfare recipient to repay me for my coerced benevolence? The way I figure it, I've been supporting welfare recipients for nearly 25 years. So why is it unreasonable to expect something in return? As a home owner I always have a yard that needs mowing, a house that needs cleaning or errands to be run.

If you're thinking that that wouldn't be reasonable, then I have to ask; why not? I had to earn it, why shouldn't they? Can't we at least require that they perform some services for the public good? I'm sure that there is plenty of trash to be picked up, roads to be built or even swamps to be drained. But no, we can't ask them to do anything, because it might be damaging to their self-esteem. Yes, I suppose they're right; there is after all much more self-esteem to be gained in sitting on your ass collecting benefits for something you didn't earn. So, I suppose all that stuff about "life, liberty, and the pursuit of happiness" was only meant for those with a vote to sell.

Putting a stop to this nonsense won't be easy and it will require some effort, but I suppose this is where the true problem lies with the Independent. The Independent, it would seem, has chosen to live the unexamined life. Thinking is a chore for him that is to be avoided at all cost. You see, thinking requires effort and those that may have once put forth the effort probably came to conclusions that they weren't entirely comfortable with. To be a real American or true Conservative doesn't just require the ability to think and come to a rational conclusion; it also means finding a solution and putting that solution to work. Yes, odds you're going to piss someone off and as such, you will need to show a little backbone, but isn't that what being an American is all about?

For many Independents, the act of thinking and forming an opinion is just too risky. Having an opinion contrary to the group often means that you could be shunned and subsequently labeled with some asinine term. Why anyone would care, I do not know. I suppose the fear of not being accepted by "the group" is just too great a burden for some to bear. So, off they go into la-la-land, pretending that their decision to be a follower will never have any real consequences.

As case-in-point, the following are just a few discussions between Liberals and so-called Independents that I have witnessed. They went something like this:

A Liberal encounter with a racist:

Liberal: I think affirmative action is a good thing, it provides opportunities to minorities who would otherwise be left out. What do you think?

Independent: I don't know...I think maybe we should all be judged on our abilities.

Liberal: I can't believe you think that—what a racist statement!

Independent: No, I just meant...

A Liberal encounter with a homophobe:

Liberal: I can't believe those Republicans are fighting against gay marriage. There's going to be a rally to support gays this weekend. Would you like to come?

Independent: Well, actually, I'm not for gay marriage either.

Liberal: Don't tell me you're a homophobe?

Independent: No, I like gay people.

A Liberal encounter with a racist homophobe:

Liberal: So, who are you voting for?

Independent: I was kind of leaning towards Bush.

Liberal: Oh my God! (This is a knee-jerk reaction only, they don't really believe in God.) You can't be serious! He's against "Hate Crimes Legislation." What are you, a Homophobic Racist?

Independent: I don't know, maybe you're right.

It should be noted that each question asked by the liberal wasn't really a solicitation for the so-called Independent's opinion. All three were loaded questions intended only to validate the liberal's position. The responses given by both are typical. Though, the responses given by the Independent in all three encounters should have gone something like this:

Independent: Have you always been a dumbass? First of all, I'm not for preferential treatment of any group. The Constitution does not recognize the rights of groups, only the rights of individuals. Secondly, to be against something doesn't make you phobic. "Phobic" means to have a fear of something. I'm also against stupidity, but that doesn't make me afraid of you.

Finally, there are already laws against individuals doing harm to others. So, why don't you tell me why it is worse to murder someone because they're gay or black, than it is to murder someone who is not? Are you telling me that their lives are worth more than others? Regardless of the murderer's reason, the punishment for the crime should be the death penalty. But, let me guess, you're probably not for that either?

Independents may claim that they are just trying to be open-minded, but the reality is they refuse to examine the facts and come to their own conclusions. If you are a so-called Independent and you cannot take it upon yourself to examine the facts, maybe the answers to the following questions will help you decide whose Party, philosophy and economic system it is that's ruining our country. They are as follows:

1. Which Party favors high rates of taxation, government control of industry and a socialized healthcare system? Answer: The Democratic Party
2. Whose Party promotes gay marriage, while denouncing Judeo-Christian values as hateful and judgmental? Answer: The Democratic Party
3. Which Party has come out against military and national interests in every conflict since the Vietnam War? Answer: The Democratic Party
4. Whose philosophy is it to assail American culture while promoting political correctness and multiculturalism? Answer: The Democrats

5. Which Party favors the United Nations control of America's domestic and foreign policy?
   Answer: The Democratic Party
6. Which Party continues to favor legislation to control or remove the right of Americans to bear arms?
   Answer: The Democratic Party
7. Whose philosophy was it that destroyed the American education system?
   Answer: The Democrats
8. And, which Party thinks you're too damn stupid to decide what is best for you and your family?
   Answer: The bloody socialist Democratic Party

Questions like these can be endless, but the answer to all is invariably the same: the Democratic Party. Any serious review of the facts will reveal the over-reaching arm of the federal government and the people behind it. All Americans must realize that a state, which controls the means of production and distribution of goods and services, also controls its citizens. As any honest Liberal or Conservative must admit, this is a point not open for debate. If it sounds like socialism and it smells like socialism, then it must be socialism!

If this is the life you desire, then go for it. Just count me out. Why any self-respecting individual would submit their life to the state, only to have the value of their existence determined by some politician or bureaucrat is beyond me. Anyone with a modicum of self-worth or pride would tell the Left to kiss their freedom-loving American ass. I try to do it every chance I get, and believe me, it's not that hard. So, screw being an Independent and try being a real American.

I'm so adamant about this that I make it a point to speak-up every time I hear some dumbass say something anti-American, and you should too. If America were truly the cause of all that is wrong in their world, then why do her critics stay? Answer: because deep down, these hypocrites realize that without the capitalist machine, their evil desires and stupid ideas could never be funded. A loser simply cannot exist without feeding off the success of others. Like a virus, without a host, the loser has no chance of survival.

As a final note to all you Independents out there who feel a person's political ideology doesn't concern you, I hope that you can remember your ambiguity when "Big Brother" is telling you how to think, where to live, what doctor to see, and how much of your wealth you should be allowed to keep. I want you to never forget how your inconsistency contributed to the downfall of capitalist America and the creation of the ever-controlling socialist state.

Also remember to ask yourself why you were more concerned with what others thought of you or why when things got tough you chose to give up your freedom in exchange for a false sense of security. Maybe then you will also realize that you were never being an Independent, just a Coward all along.

Chapter 5

Capitalism vs. Socialism

"If you destroy a free market, you create a black market." Sir Winston Churchill

C apitalism vs. socialism—the superiority of the former over the latter is evident in the fact that it is only the former that can exist on it's own merits, while the latter (socialism) requires the forced acceptance of not only its detractors, but the support of the very system (capitalism) it attempts to depose. And yet, socialists are still insistent that it is the capitalist that is insensitive and indifferent to the plight of people. While there may be some truth to this claim, the Left's perception of why has no basis in reality. To believe that personal failure in a competitive system is somehow an indictment on capitalism is no more a notion founded in reality, than communism is a success because everyone is equally miserable.

The reality is that capitalism is superior for the very reasons the envy-ridden fools abhor it. Whether they choose to accept it or not, the fact that someone will lose is actually a good thing. Their false perception of capitalism is also the reason why the government now considers itself the arbiter of fairness. While only one of life's losers could perceive the forced transference of property from one person to another as fair, the reality is that socialism is nothing more than government sanctioned theft.

While most Americans tend to view failure and loss as only a temporary state, the Left has decided that no achiever shall go unpunished for their accomplishments. In their perverted feel-good world, everyone deserves a trophy. Whether by taxation, mandate or regulation the accomplished must not go un-punished. Even if we were not to consider all evidence and empirical data, you would think that America's success in such a relatively short period of time would be enough to convince them otherwise.

For those who refuse to accept that men and not governments are responsible for their station in life, I'll explain. First, any claim that capitalism is unfair is a contention based on nothing short of ignorance, stupidity, envy, collective greed, cowardice, laziness, corruptness, and/or utter incompetence. All of which, by-the-way, have nothing to do with capitalism and everything to do with poor character. The truth of the matter is that it is the Left's acceptance of mediocrity and outright promotion of victimhood that prevents them from understanding the truth about capitalism.

What is this truth I speak of, this friend of the environment, of both sexes and of all races, creeds and nationalities? Drum roll please! Why, it's none other than efficiency. Capitalism and efficiency are inseparable as each relies on the other to foster competition in free, fair and open markets. You might say that efficiency is to capitalism what inefficiency is to socialism. Because individuals are free to choose in a capitalist system, competitors are always faced with the reality of finding more efficient means of production in order to compete. With socialism, competition is discouraged and thus efficiencies can seldom if ever develop.

Because capitalism allows men to act on their own behalf, it is usually the person or company who is most efficient and innovative that wins. Still, having lost in a competitive situation doesn't necessarily make you one of life's losers. The transition into being one of life's losers either occurs when you decide to quit or when in order to win in the market, you look to the government or others for satisfaction. In essence, you have chosen to give up and direct your efforts towards seeking an equality of results through protest as opposed to competition. Any positive result gained from such protests is an indictment on socialism, not capitalism. In a true capitalist system, there is no such thing as luck, unless you define luck as opportunity taken advantage of by those prepared for it.

The fact that failure happens, and losses occur, is a reality that the productive accept. You see, for the productive, having lost can be the very thing that compels them to continue competing and striving towards a win. It is from this strong motivation to win that efficiencies are created and perseverance is ultimately rewarded. Still, before a product or service can become more efficient, individuals and businesses have to be innovative. The individuals and businesses who continue to innovate and find efficiencies will be the ones who are rewarded with greater market share and improved profit margins—and making a buck is a good thing. After all, if a Capitalist never made a buck, a Socialist wouldn't have anyone to steal it from.

For an example of efficiency at work, choose any current industry in America. Do automotive and computer manufacturers not come out with new and improved products each year and generally at lower prices? When you consider the costs of goods and services on an inflation adjusted basis this is especially true. When adjusted for inflation, did you know that the price of an average personal computer in 2008 is cheaper than the first hand-held calculators produced in the 1970s?

Even the environment benefits from capitalism. To understand how, you need only to imagine any economy without competition. Believe me, it wouldn't take any stretch of the imagination to say that nearly every product or service produced in a non competitive system would be crap. Think about it! When products are designed and built like crap, do they not have to be replaced more often? What do you suppose it means to the environment when a consumer has no choice and a company is allowed to consistently produce more crap?

What it means is that more raw materials and energy will be needed to produce more crap that will never reach its potential or meet consumer expectations. Now, doesn't every good little environmentalist want to avoid the unnecessary overuse of raw materials and energy? Consider also, that without competition there would never be a newer "longer lasting", "less expensive" or "more efficient" model of anything created. How can it not be obvious to even the loser that competition is a good thing, even for him?

Whether by design, or sheer stupidity, the Left simply refuses to accept that without competition the world would be an extremely inefficient and wasteful place. Just take a nice hard look at every commie-pinko nation that has ever existed and you'll see that were it not for an efficient and open market, we too would be driving inefficient crappy little cars like the East

German Trabant and standing in long lines for sub-standard goods and services. To all you leftists who never made the pilgrimage to the former communist East Germany, a Trabant is a crappy little commie car powered by a two-cycle engine that produces more pollution than 20 American SUVs. Not to mention, it has the suspension of a go-cart and less room than the back seat of a Pinto. As an even greater example of communist efficiency, the average East German had to wait twelve years to get the little piece of crap.

It would be easy to say that the they have failed yet again in their illogical train of thought, but that would assume some thought had gone into their claims against capitalism to begin with. As harsh as it may sound, it is simply not the task of capitalism to make anyone successful. But, by the same token it is not the fault of capitalism that someone has failed either. To say that "capitalism is a horrible economic system," because some have failed is utterly moronic. Achievement has everything to do with the individual and nothing to do with an economic system that is indifferent to anyone's feelings. Capitalism's only task is to provide for a free and open economy allowing equal access to all legal parties. Granted, equal access to the marketplace does not mean or guarantee equal results; superior marketing, limited regulation and open distribution channels can be just as crucial.

When individuals are free to act on their own behalf, it isn't greed that inspires most; it is their desire to succeed. Whether you define it as self-esteem or as having an ego, it is simply part of the human condition that many are motivated to excel. How else could one explain the inferiority of goods and services produced by communist countries? Any economic or social system that robs men of their ego, provides no incentive for men to excel. This is especially true in countries where individual achievement is discouraged and any progress made is viewed as a collective achievement.

If you think I'm full of it, then tell me what of great significance has come out of Africa, China, Russia, South America, third-world Asia or the Middle East? Why is it that in almost all of these regions advanced technological products have to be imported or reverse engineered? I can't think of a single thing in the last two hundred years that any of these regions have created or produced of technological significance.

For that matter, when was the last time you bought a quality product from Russia, North Korea, Cuba, or Vietnam? No, I didn't forget China. China is somewhat of a paradox. It is certainly a communist country, but unlike other communist regimes, they have realized—whether they'll admit it or not—that communism as an economic system is a failure. Sure it works great in oppressing people, but it's a real bitch when production numbers can't be met and over a billion people need to be fed.

To improve its economic position, China had no choice but to embrace—though in small part—some free market reforms. Still, before you get too excited, you should know that their motives were more in the interests of their government and not that of their people. Much like our own leftists, the Chi-Coms simply realized that sometimes you need to induce people to produce at higher levels, even if it means throwing them a bone every now and then by letting them keep a little of what they earned.

It is a fact, that most modern technology found in communist, fascist or theocratic nations today came from West or as a result of Western technological advancements. It is also a fact that much of the West's technology has been stolen by way of patent infringement, corporate theft, spying, copyright violations and/or campaign contributions to the Democratic Party by these same vile governments. And, before you begin to think that China has made great strides, remember that there are no OSHA standards and slave labor is still very common. The increase in profit margins taken from the use of zero to low cost labor simply allows the Chi-Coms even greater opportunities to develop more weapons and purchase more US secrets; at least when Democrats are in power.

As with other communist and socialist regimes, communist China does not allow individuals to wholly benefit from their achievements. Individual achievement is seen as a collective accomplishment and worthy only if it benefits the state. Such action taken against individuals only serves to rob them of their incentive to achieve. In the 20th century Thomas Edison, Henry Ford, Willis Carrier, the Wright Brothers, and Steve Jobs accomplished something no government, large corporation, or other group entity ever had. Their inventions not only created millions of new jobs, but also added comfort, leisure and longevity to the lives of billions.

The invention and mass production of light bulbs, automobiles, air conditioners, airplanes and computers all came about without the help or interference of the federal government. These inventions also inspired countless others which helped to kick-off an explosion in Western technological advancements. Consider what might have happened if the US government had interfered by demanding that no man would be allowed to benefit from his own thoughts and ideas? Where do you suppose we would be today without artificial light, mass produced transportation, refrigeration, or rapid forms of communication? Does anyone really believe that the federal government is capable of creating, generating and delivering goods and services in a timely an efficient manner?

Capitalism, when practiced among moral men, and within a society that respects the rule of law is inferior to none. The underachiever's inability has nothing to do with capitalism and everything to do with personal fortitude. It is the underachiever's unwilling attitude that has created his lot in life and the fact that he finds his lot in life to be undesirable is of no consequence to capitalism. Next time you hear some dumbass knock capitalism, you should ask for an example of where capitalism has ever prevented someone from following their dream. Beyond the usual incoherent leftist nonsense, do not expect a logical or reasonable answer.

If given its proper due, it can even be said of capitalism that it is the epitome of freedom, as it is the only viable economic system known to man that does not seek to deprive him of his life, liberty and property. Now contrast that with socialism, whose only goal it is to deprive men of their individual value and unalienable rights through government controls. Whether practiced by a democratic, theocratic, communist or fascist regime, socialism in any capacity grants governments powers none have a natural right to.

I've read the Declaration of Independence and the Constitution several times, and nowhere in either document does it state or intimate in even the slightest way that the prosperous shall be obligated to forfeit a disproportionate amount of their wealth to the non-productive. If the left truly believed in equality for all, they would support the flat-tax system over the inequality of the progressive tax system that robs so many people today of their freedom and property. Why should a person earning $100,000 a year pay a much higher rate than someone earning $25,000? Especially when you consider that the person making the higher salary will most likely never receive—much less be entitled to—the same welfare benefits? Is this not prejudicial? So, is it fair that the government-defined rich get to pay 97% of all taxes and receive little or no return on the confiscation of their wealth?

So much for the pursuit of happiness! Sounds more like the pursuit of extortion to me. You don't think its extortion; then consider one of the Left's most prominent arguments on behalf of welfare. It is the position of many on the Left that if welfare did not exist there would be mass rioting, starvation and chaos in the streets. Think about that! What they're saying is; that we have no other choice but to feed, house, transport, educate, medicate and clothe the irresponsible lest we have our own belongings or life taken from us. It must really piss off the mafia to see the Federal government blatantly getting away with extortion, when so many of them have gone to jail for the same offense.

When the Constitution states that we are "created equal" that's what it means. "Created" only implies that at life's inception, everyone shares the same unalienable rights. So, whatever your plight may be, it is not America's fault, but rest assured you have the same rights as all other Americans. The point is, you are here and what you choose to do with your life is your responsibility. Since the dawn of man's existence it has been his natural condition to accept responsibility for himself. After all, which is truly more selfish, serving yourself or expecting others to serve you?

Maybe the following scenario will help to clarify my point:

Imagine if you will, a simpler time in America, a time when most Americans relied primarily on an agrarian-based economy. Assume also that you own 40 acres of farmland, land you toil over sixteen hours a day during the growing season to support your family and stock up for the winter.

Suppose also that the 40-acre tract next to you was recently inherited by the shiftless son of your deceased neighbor. And, rather than spend his time working the farm he chose to hang out at the local tavern getting drunk and withering away his inheritance.

Now envision that one evening while sitting by the fire smoking your pipe you are interrupted by a knock at the door. Turning to the little lady busy stirring up a pot of hot potato stew you ask, "Who could that be at such an hour?" After answering the door, you find that it is the shiftless heir of your deceased neighbor drunk from his over indulgence of ale.

Upon asking him what it is that he wants at such and hour, he responds that he is cold and hungry, and having no wood to burn for heat or food to cook, he requires both a meal and shelter for the evening. Not sensing your obvious agitation at being interrupted or of being asked to provide these things to him, he goes on to insist that it is your moral duty to provide these things for him.

Knowing full well of his slothful ways, still you tell him no and that he is not welcome. In response he tells you how selfish you are for not sharing with him your good fortune. Unrelenting, he even insists that you owe him a hot meal and warmth for the evening. He then goes on to tell you that he would not be in this predicament had his father been able to afford a doctor to lance his boils and bleed him.

You, failing to see the logic in his argument, begin reaching for the flintlock perched atop the mantle. He then, realizing your intent to defend your property, begins his hasty retreat, all the while screaming for gun control and national healthcare.

I have no doubt in my mind that this is how such a scenario would have played out. So, if a man's common sense would have prevented him from being taken advantage of then, why can't it now? And, if it wasn't possible for the worthless to steal from their productive neighbors then, why should it be now? If you're among the unthinking and believe that because it was a much simpler time and people had no choice, then you're not only an idiot, but a sap as well. Yes, times may have been simpler, but are we so sophisticated that we must allow ourselves to be taken advantage of by the dregs of society or by their proxies who wish nothing more than to rule over us?

We should demand much more from those who wish to live off the backs of others and of the elected who proclaim a change and a vision of the future. If that future doesn't include the full and complete recognition of life, liberty and property, then they should be told to go to hell. When our government seeks to control our lives to its benefit, it is the responsibility of every true-American to stop those who would seek to oppress us, either by vote or force.

The prior story also illustrated one of the primary reasons why our Constitution is compatible with capitalism and why both are necessary to the success of our Nation. You see, the farmer's unalienable right to bear arms secured his right to the ownership of his property, which in turn allowed him to produce sustenance for his family. In any socialist system of government the farmer would not have had these rights. In a collective state he would have had no individual rights and his needs would have been secondary to the needs of his worthless neighbor.

Though the Constitution has made it quite clear that all men are created equal and that men are responsible for themselves and their actions, they continue unabated in their quest to either revise the Constitution or to abolish it altogether. If you cannot accept that the Constitution means what it says and that capitalism is superior to all other economic systems, then you are doomed to your own falsity in life.

C. S. Lewis made a great point when he wrote of liberalism decades ago. Referring to a liberal as, "The modern democratic planner, and mild-eyed scientist [...]" he wrote:

> "He believes that 'good' means whatever men are conditioned to approve. He believes that it is the function of him and his kind to condition men; to create conscientiousness by eugenics, psychological manipulation of infants, state education and mass propaganda."

I think he may have just hit the nail right on the head with that one.

Chapter 6

Dumbing it Down

"Justice Breyer proceeds on the erroneous and all-too-common assumption that the Constitution means what we think it ought to mean. It does not; it means what it says." Antonin Scalia, Supreme Court Justice

As best as I can recollect, it was only the unabridged version of American history that was taught during my primary and secondary school years. Yes, a history no doubt taught from an American perspective, but why shouldn't it have been? Unlike the Left, I don't particularly care what our enemies think of us, much less what their version of history is. To the victors go the spoils! Well, so too does their version of past events and if those events happen to be a bit skewed, bellicose or romanticized for the sake of national pride, I certainly don't care. Besides, if I have to hear how proud certain non-Americans are of their unaccomplished cultures, why can't I be proud of the most accomplished culture in the history of mankind?

Whatever their reasons are for despising America's past and loathing its present, I don't care, because I don't believe alleged American greed, selfishness or arrogance has a damn thing to do with how others conduct themselves around the world. The facts are that America is a great and wonderful country and that the world is a hell-of-a-lot better off because of her. The Left's disloyalty and self-serving charges certainly don't merit a rewriting of American history either—no matter how guilty they may feel or what they hope to accomplish socially or economically. So excuse me if I don't feel the least bit guilty or agreeable to the political agenda of a bunch of 60's era socialists.

You know, it has always been a favored tactic of collectivist regimes to rewrite their nation's history. Whether for purposes of erasing the past or creating a mythical present, countries such as; Germany, Japan, Italy, Russia and China have all rewritten parts of their history to promote economic schemes and make acceptable State sponsored terror. I suppose it's only because we're much nicer than they were that our government has chosen to take a more subtle approach. I suppose also that that whole genocide thing of the 30s, 40s, and 50s must have lost its appeal. Still, I think someone ought to inform the Middle East and Africa that such actions have become passé.

Nevertheless, our government has been quite busy at re-writing our history. Sure they have been much more subtle and have been doing so incrementally, but it is happening. Don't believe me, then consider for just a moment what's going on with education, immigration and the judicial system. Have entire parts of our Nation's history not been removed from the text books of primary and secondary schools? Are our schools not more concerned with teaching multiculturalism and self-esteem today than they are with teaching the fundamentals? What do you think the affect will be if we grant Amnesty to 22 million illegal aliens? Do you think that even a minority of them will understand their Oath to the Constitution much less be willing to defend it? And why is it that Judges now have the power to mandate curriculums or determine funding?

For now, my claims may seem baseless, but as with many things in life that matter, you can only look the other way for so long. For me, it happened when my eldest son brought home his first so-called history book. From that point on I could look no other way, but to the fools who were propagating anti-Americanism. Following a cursory review of this book's content, the first words out of my mouth were literally, "You've got to be shittin' me!" This so-called history book, as with all others that followed, weren't even written by American historians, they were all written by idiots with education degrees.

Had it not been for the books in my home, written by real historians, my sons may have been brainwashed into believing Che Guevara was merely a freedom fighter or that Nelson Mandela was some great democratic leader and not a communist. Or even that Maya Angelou was the greatest poet the West had ever known and not a hack simply regurgitating the obvious, albeit with the greatest amount of philosophical hypocrisy. Worse yet, they may have come to believe that it was soviet Premier Mikhail Gorbachev that hastened the end of communism in Russia and not President Ronald Reagan.

Because dealing with such leftist stupidity on a daily basis can be taxing (pun intended) on the mind, I find myself often daydreaming of an America where government's influence and control of our lives is as it should be—limited. Because my daydreams are often of a political nature too, moments of brilliance occur often enough for me to also solve many of the world's problems. In fact, it was during one of my daydreams that I got to wondering what our Founding Fathers might have done differently had they known so many dumbasses would come to dominate the American political system.

While they could not have known or even imagined the likes of a Ted Kennedy or a Bill Clinton being anything more than a town drunk and a local charlatan, they might still have taken steps to prevent the influence of their ideology on American culture. Really now, who of us hasn't wondered what the world might be like if we could travel back in time to change the course of history. Certainly there are those of us who would want to prevent horrific events by assassinating some of history's greatest villains, and there are those that might even want to save a loved one from some unfortunate fate. But, wouldn't it also be great if we could warn our Forefathers of the impending dangers posed by today's dumbasses? Consider how different the debate might be today had the Founding Fathers been more explicit or detailed in their writings. Sure, it may have been common sense then, but for our dumbed-down culture it is little more than Greek.

Unlike those who seem to dwell in fantasy land, I know that time travel is not possible, but what might have been done more than 200 years ago may still be possible today, if only we have enough men of character willing to reaffirm their original intent. Dumbing down both the Constitution and Declaration of Independence might seem drastic, but at a minimum it would force its detractors to be honest about where they stand. The otherwise useless and stupid might also wise up once they learn how they have been lied to. Of course, if such action was taken, the Left would probably be forced to implement their version of the "final solution," that is, to insist that people not be allowed to read or write.

Needless to say, you and I both know that even if we were successful at amending or rewriting certain portions of our founding documents on a level that most liberals could understand, it probably wouldn't matter—because the true argument here isn't what the words mean, but whether those words in their entirety have any meaning at all to liberals. Still, I believe that at a minimum, liberals would be forced to be honest about their position, as there would be no doubt as to the true meaning of our founding documents.

The purpose of my revisions would only be meant to clarify to all Americans that any elected government who chooses to deviate from or act contrary to the express intent of the founding documents could be rightfully removed by the people. While I do not think it would be reasonable to hold liberal contempt, in and of itself sufficient to merit such action, once their verbal contempt turned to clear unconstitutional actions, those detractors would have to be dealt with severely. While judges, politicians and various government bureaucracies have already acted unconstitutionally by legislating from the bench, overriding the will of the people or mandating unlawful rules and regulations, we Americans have done little to stop them.

If our Forefathers could have foreseen the lunacy of the Federal government to come, I am confident that our founding documents might have rivaled the length of War and Peace. Each word, phrase, and dangling participle might have to have been explained so that the common-sense-impaired could understand their express meaning. Can you imagine Adams and Jefferson sitting down to write The Declaration of Independence and getting caught up in what the true meaning of "is" is?

Liberals may want us to believe that words lose their meaning and substance over time, but if we adhered to their logic, documents and contracts written today would be worthless tomorrow. Additionally, if we were to accept their "Living Breathing Document" theory, men would be bound by no law, subject only to theirs' and others' whims. If taken to the extreme, no contract in America would be worth the paper it is written on. America would be a country full of charlatans and thugs worse even than most members of both the Democratic and Republican Parties.

Now you might be thinking that I'm being a bit hypocritical by suggesting that we make some changes to our founding documents, but that's not the case at all. It is every bit my intention to leave them in their original state. I'm only suggesting that we provide footnotes to the text to assist those who lack a basic understanding of the English language and/or who fail to grasp any inference or inflection when one is made. By doing so, there would hopefully be no question as to what these documents mean and what our Founding Fathers had hoped to accomplish.

To show just how easy this would be, the following are just a few recommendations we might consider to help the mentally deficient among us understand. Let's begin with what I consider to be America's first official document, The Declaration of Independence:

"WHEN in the course of human Events, it becomes necessary for one People to dissolve the Political Bands which have connected them with another, and to assume among the Powers of the Earth, the separate and equal Station to which the Laws of Nature and of Nature's God entitle them, a decent Respect to the Opinions of Mankind requires that they should declare the causes which impel them to the Separation.

WE hold these truths to be self evident, that all men are created equal...[1]"

[1]*When we say, "created equal," we mean just that. "Created" implies the beginning and only the beginning. It does not mean each man will remain equal in wealth and stature throughout his life. Every man progresses at his own self-prescribed rate; that is, what you choose to do with your life is your decision and no one else's. You are responsible for yourself. You will not be asked to assume another's responsibility, only to accept your own.*

"But when a long Train of Abuses and Usurpations, pursuing invariably the same Object, evinces a Design to reduce them under absolute Despotism, it is their Right, it is their Duty, to throw off such Government, and to provide new Guards for their future Security. Such has been the patient Sufferance of these colonies;...[2]"

[2]*What is meant by this statement is that when a government becomes oppressive, it is the duty and the right of the people to dissolve such a government by whatever means possible. In the case of our Forefathers, it was to take up arms against the King of England who had sought to oppress them. When events necessitate immediate action, each American citizen is endowed by his Creator to act in his own interest and to confront those who seek to oppress him. In order for the Republic to survive, citizens are allowed to defend themselves against criminal forces whether they are individuals or government entities.*

After reading this footnote, it should be easy to understand why the Founding Fathers created the Second Amendment to the Constitution. And, now that we have made the leap to the Constitution, we might as well begin with its preamble as well, which states:

"We the People of the United States, in Order to form a more perfect Union, establish Justice, insure domestic Tranquility, provide for the common defense, promote the general Welfare, and secure the Blessings of Liberty to ourselves and our Posterity, do ordain and establish this Constitution for the United States of America.[1]"

> [1]*What is meant in this statement is that a government of the people and by the people derives its just powers from only the people. If you will, it simply means that the government exists only to the extent that it acts in the interests of preserving individual rights. It does not mean that the government has the right to transfer wealth from one citizen to another. Or to favor one industry over another, enjoin with foreign governments against its citizenry or to suspend any unalienable right recognized by the Constitution.*

Let's focus now on a few specific Amendments enumerated in the Bill of Rights, as it is here—albeit incorrectly—that the Left claims to have special insight into. It is also here that many Americans are most familiar with what little they do know of their Constitution.

The First Amendment

"Congress shall make no law respecting an establishment of religion, or prohibiting the free exercise thereof;[1] or abridging the freedom of speech, or of the press;[2] or the right of the people peaceably to assemble, and to petition the Government for a redress of grievances.[3]"

> [1]*Though congress shall make no law respecting the establishment of religion, it does not also seek to separate the church entirely from the state. This would not be possible as the very foundation of our Nation and its laws is rooted in the Judeo-Christian faith.*
>
> [2]*Though each citizen and the press shall have the right to freedom of speech, no citizen or organization shall be exempt from the responsibility it requires, meaning that each shall remain subject to the laws of libel and slander or other reckless and malicious intent.*

³Though it is the exclusive right of the people to peaceably assemble, it is not their right to do so on privately held property nor is it their right to do so on publicly owned property when the express intent of their assembly is to impede commerce, prevent the safe movement of citizens or to obstruct a lawful and just (Constitutional) government.

The Second Amendment

"A well-regulated Militia, being necessary to the security of a Free State, the right of the people to keep and bear Arms, shall not be infringed.[4] "

⁴Two separate and express statements have been made in the 2nd Amendment. The first statement refers only to the protection of the states against foreign enemies and the provisions of common defense for an organized and well-regulated militia. The second statement within this compound/complex sentence is meant to clarify to all local, state, and federal governments that individuals reserve the exclusive right to bear arms in order to protect their life, liberty, and property, and if they so desire, to keep arms on their person for such security.

As for all other Amendments, well you get the picture. With a little applied common sense the same could be done for all. Though it was not one of the original Ten Amendments ratified, had the 16th Amendment been included among those proposed in the original Bill of Rights, I am sure of one thing; The Constitution would never have been ratified with its inclusion. Though the Sixteenth Amendment was not ratified until 1913, the following is how I believe many of the Founding Fathers would have responded had it been offered as an Amendment in 1789.

The Sixteenth Amendment

"The Congress shall have power to lay and collect taxes on incomes, from whatever source derived, without apportionment among the several States, and without regard to any census or enumeration."

Their Probable Response:

The Amendment to create a National Income Tax is an abomination of the highest sorts and an insult to the purpose of this assembly—it is not now nor shall it ever be the intention of the United States of America to put upon its citizens a tax that would serve to benefit only some, while ceding to the Federal government a power that might not be restrained. Such an Amendment would not only be an affront to man's liberty, but would also act as an unnatural barrier to the ways of men since it serves only to set citizens in opposition to one another. Man's desire should be in the pursuit of life, liberty, and happiness, not of his neighbor's wealth. As is clearly stated in the 10th Amendment; "The powers not delegated to the United States by the Constitution, nor prohibited by it to the States, are reserved to the States respectively, or to the people."

Should a State wish to levy a tax on income of any sort, let it be their affair to do so. An amendment of this sort would make acceptable a right of the Federal government to levy taxes on the productive citizens of these many States for the benefit of itself and others, others who might not ever share in the costs. Such a tax might also give rise to allegiances between the elected and the non-productive. What manner of protection will then be guaranteed the productive individual in such an instance? How can an amendment be justified that would put upon some the burden of others? Is it the Federal government's duty to force the benevolence of others in matters of supposed social justice? It is plain to see that such an amendment would only serve to punish the productive citizens of these United States.

For those who think that this is just another right-wing rant, I ask you to think again. Yes, I do despise socialism in all its variants, but this misguided ideology is not my only inspiration. With stupidity in such abundance these days, it would be tough to reserve my thoughts solely for leftist movement? My contempt is for anyone whose goal it is to diminish American sovereignty and individual liberty and that includes so-called conservatives masquerading as strict Constitutionalists. The focus of this book is on the whole of collectivist ideology in all its forms. Should you think next that I am just another right wing extremist trying to impose his Christian ideology on others, you would be wrong yet again.

In the Christian faith, it is said that we are all born in sin, and I suppose my hate for some and displeasure for others would make me a considerable sinner. It is a fault I simply cannot elude—I despise evil and I believe most collectivist ideologies to be evil, even if its purveyors have good intentions or are ignorant of its consequences. That said, I do not believe all leftists to be entirely evil. I understand that some may only suffer from temporary stupidity; you know, the type you get from being indoctrinated at school or brainwashed by the media. It is altogether probable that many of these people will someday snap out of it; at least once they get a real job. So, I suppose there is hope for some to one day become real Americans.

Chapter 7

Mohammed and the Girls Next Door

"O you who believe! Do not take the Jews and Christians for friends; they are friends of each other; and whoever amongst you takes them for a friend, then surely he is one of them; surely Allah does not guide the unjust people." Quran: [5.51]

Since the terrorist acts of 9/11, I can't even begin to tell you how many times I have heard some idiot say that it might never have happened, had we only understood why they hated us. What a load of crap. Just where in the hell have these people been for the last 30 years? They hate us because we're pro-Israel, pro-democracy, women and oh yeah, we refuse to submit to Islam. There, do you feel any safer now? Or are you ready to throw in the towel and change your Western beliefs?

Well, I'm not about to change my beliefs or American ways for any gang of brainwashed murderous psychopaths or anyone else for that matter. If I wanted to change, I'd move to one of the many rat-hole nations that comprise the Middle East, Third World Asia, or Africa, and join the cultic merriment of bashing the U.S. and Israel. The wussified Left may think that we need to understand where all the rage comes from, but let me tell you something, we no more need to understand Islam's neurotic psychosis than we do Bill Clinton's penchant for chubby white chicks.

If I hear one more idiot insinuate Americans are stupid because they're unaware of the world around them, I might just have to open-up a Texas size can of whoop-ass on them. Besides, if we are so stupid, then why are so many of the world's so-called smart people trying to come here? So, if anyone needs to learn anything, it would be America's detractors, and they could start by learning how to bathe and be civilized. Other than living in squalor, acting like savages, screaming like little girls, murdering and torturing people for speaking their minds, or allowing some scumbag to control every facet of their life, I just can't see what it is that they have to teach us.

So, just what is it that makes the Muslim world or any other group so special that Americans should even care what they think about us? We're told that the majority of Europeans and Asians hate us as well; should we bother to change for them too? If we betrayed our predominant faith and converted to Islam, would that mean that the Europeans would then like us? What if we decided to fully embrace socialism and act like the smelly French—would that mean anyone would like us? Really, I'm baffled as to why any American would care why these ingrates hate us.

Let's assume for just a moment that you do give a rat's ass about why they loathe us; would you then be willing to change your core beliefs and adopt another culture? I'm not talking about America's leftists—they've already sold their souls to the hordes of "Blame America First" trash. Hell, many of them are even leading the charge. What I want to know, is whether real Americans are willing to change their way of life to satisfy the collective envy of others?

If you really don't understand why so many in the world hate and despise us and don't want to waste your time listening to all their anti-America rants to find out, I'll save you the time and trouble. They hate us for the same reason some ugly people hate pretty people and why some poor people hate the rich and even why some stupid people hate smart people: envy. So, there it is... your question has been answered.

Yes, the answer is just that simple. I hate to burst the bubble of all those over-educated and common-sense-impaired yahoos at the State Department and on college campuses across the country, but it is truly that simple. If you don't believe me, it must be because: 1) you haven't been paying attention; 2) you have no basic understanding of human nature; or 3) it makes you feel superior to over intellectualize the obvious.

All that said, if a more complex answer will let you sleep better at night, I'll break it down for you. First, to understand Islam's hate of the West, we'll need to start at the beginning, which means that we will need to start with its founder, Mohammed. Thanks to modern-day psychology (developed by the West) we can judge Mohammed based on his actions and the tenets of the faith he created. Once I'm finished, you should arrive at the same conclusion that I have. Which is that by any clinical standards of today, Mohammed would be diagnosed a sociopath. So, let's get started.

As most people of faith today are familiar with the stories of the Old and New Testament, so too were the many people of the Middle East living during the seventh century. Mohammed was no exception either. In fact, much that is written in both the Old and New Testament can be found in the Koran. I haven't read the entire Koran, but apart from the infidel bashing and its addendum, the Shari' a (the book of Islamic law), the content and tone is somewhat similar to that of the Old and New Testament.

With Christians, Jews and Muslims sharing many of the same tenets, you may be wondering what all the fighting is about. Especially since we can't turn on the news today without hearing how Islam is a "religion of peace." Peace? It's a piece of something alright, but peaceful it aint. Since you're not likely to hear it from the press, let me enlighten you as to some of the ways Muslims are instructed by the Koran to treat Jews and non-believers. According to the Koran, the Jew and non-believer must be enslaved, taxed or put to death for his refusal to convert to Islam. Based on historical accounts, the choice taken, usually depended only on what was most beneficial to Islam at the time. It was from this edict and many others like it found throughout the Koran that I was able to deduce that neither the Christian nor Jewish faith was to Mohammed's liking.

So what's a wannabe prophet to do, but create his own religion? Of course, if you are an illiterate nut-job, you will need some help. So, with the Old and New Testament as their guide, and with a proclamation here and there by Mohammed, he and his scribes forged a new faith. And by forge I mean; murdered, raped, pillaged and plundered all who would not submit and even some who did.

While I'm sure Mohammed had his own vision of what he wanted his new faith to be, what he still needed was something to make it believable. So, around 700 A.D. Mohammed was mysteriously visited by the archangel Gabriel, who came with nothing less than a message from God, at least so he proclaimed.

And, based on the success of the first message, there would be several more to come. Yes, a new religion had been born and it wouldn't be long before Mohammed and friends were tearing-up the desert sands in the tradition of the Mongol hordes. Again, I'm no expert on Islam, but I'm going to take what I do know and apply nothing less than my common sense.

From just the few facts I've given you, you should have learned that Islam is not a religion compatible with the ideas of the West. If a religion cannot accept that men have free-will, it cannot recognize that men are born with certain unalienable rights either. It is simply not possible for a devout Muslim to follow the tenets of Islam and live a life of freedom. Because his allegiance is to Islam only, individualism remains an obscure thought at best. Since the Constitution of the United States guarantees religious freedom and Islam does not, the two cannot coexist. Within the Muslim world; politics, culture and economics are inseparable, and all are bound together solely by Islam. Every Muslim state is either ruled in part or whole by religious authorities and every decision is based on Islamic (religious) law.

Like Christianity and Judaism, Islam too has many sects. Though, unlike Christianity and Judaism, these sects can't seem to get along with one another. The two major sects of Islam are Sunni and Shiite and both detest one another, so much so that when they're not busy murdering innocent Christians and Jews, they're killing one another. The only thing either can agree on is that all Jews and most Christians must die. As odd as it may seem, Muslims have made certain exceptions for Christians, at least for those who have something to offer in the areas of new technology, production and/or wealth. Apparently, the fact that Jews have won the Nobel Prize for science more than any other ethnic group is of little significance to Islam.

Much like that of the Democratic Party's elite, Islam's religious leaders prefer a climate of instability to maintain their power. An example of this might be an edict given by a religious leader that sets one sect against another. If this fails to create internal strife, sectarian violence or war, well there's always the West to blame for something. Many Muslims are so unyielding in their beliefs that they will go as far as to murder family members whose beliefs do not comport with their own. With every aspect of a Muslim's life being determined for him it is easy to see how there is no room for individualism. Sure, some have attempted to challenge religious authority and I commend them—but for those not lucky enough to escape persecution, their fate is usually imprisonment, torture and even death.

To further understand the cultural differences that separate Islam from the West, let's look at some of their more common practices. For example, take the fact that in some Islamic sects, the culturally inferior practice of clitorectomies still occurs. This grotesque act is commonly carried out by the girl's own mother and usually with the help of several friends to hold the screaming child down. I'll give you a moment now to collect yourself. I still need one every time I read or hear about this savagery. While baffled as to how such a barbaric tradition could even get started, I once again—though only after considerable thought—came to a conclusion that is entirely probable. As this is a tradition that has been passed down in the Islamic faith for hundreds of years, it could be surmised that it may have been started by one of Islam's founders.

Whoever it was, he certainly must have been a self-repressed sexually sick son-of-a-bitch with major feelings of inadequacy. Again, thanks to the quasi-science of psychology, and some Freudian insight, it seems that someone may have been incapable of "taking care of business," if you know what I mean. By way of regressive (historical) psychoanalysis, I came-up with a scenario that while it may be greatly speculative, it is highly probable that it may have taken place in a tent, in the middle of a desert, somewhere in the Middle East, some 13 centuries ago.

Act I – Mohammed Speaks

Mohammed: Thank you, my brothers for joining me today in my tent. Tonight we will feast and rejoice in our conquests. Peace be upon you.

Ali: Yes, our conquests there have been many. Peace be upon you.

Ahmed: Yes, I too, have had many conquests. Peace be upon you.

Mohammed: Soon, we will push the evil Christians and Jews into the sea and rejoice at their pain and suffering.

Ali: (Whispering to Ahmed) What is he talking about? I thought we were talking about chicks.

Ahmed: (Whispering back) I don't know.

Mohammed: Yes, my brothers, soon we will lead our armies to the ends of the Earth and destroy all those who refuse the word of Allah.

Ali: Aaaa! Mohammed, I thought we were talking about chicks.

Ahmed: Yes, chicks. This is very good.

Mohammed: What are you fools talking about?

Ali: Dude, check it out! Last week after my twelfth marriage, I had sex six times in one evening and my newest bride counted no less than six orgasms.

Ahmed: (Speaking with usual male bravado) Oh, Silly Ali! That is nothing. Why, just last night I gave three of my youngest wives no less than four orgasms each. I believe this doubles the amount of orgasms you've given, my friend.

Mohammed: Shut up, you idiots! What are you talking about? Curses on your mustaches!

Ahmed: A thousand apologies, Mohammed. Of course, this is your tent. How rude of us for speaking out of turn. We have no doubt that you have caused many a lady to fall prey to your sword, if you know what I mean. Tell us, oh Great One, what is your record—would it be 18, 36, maybe 72?

Mohammed: Aaaaaa, yes! It is 72, now shut up you fools and listen.

Puzzled and distracted by Ali and Ahmed's comments, Mohammed decides to retire for the evening. The next morning, Mohammed summons Ali and Ahmed back to his tent to discuss recent revelations.

Act II – Mohammed Has a Visitor

Mohammed: My Brothers, last night Allah came to me in my dreams and put forth two decrees. First, any man who dies in the name of jihad shall receive 72 virgins in paradise. You will notice that this matches my record for orgasms given to the ladies and once it is written there can be no refuting it. As it is said, so it shall be written.

Ali: Sweet!

Ahmed: Cool!

Mohammed: Shut up and listen, you fools! Secondly, women shall no longer be allowed the pleasure of an orgasm. Their sinful ways have displeased Allah. And, to ensure that orgasms no longer occur, the clitoris of every woman shall be removed.

Ali: (Whispering to Ahmed) I knew that camel-humping bastard was lying. There's no way in hell he gave 72 orgasms in one night!

Ahmed: Dude, we're screwed.

Now, if you think I'm some Redneck that has never been out of the state of Texas, let me set you straight on another thing. I've been to Saudi Arabia, Bahrain, Mexico, and five different European countries. In fact, I spent a lovely four months in Saudi while in the Air Force during Operation "Southern Watch" and let me tell you I got to witness some pretty strange things. For instance, it is against the law in the Kingdom of Saudi Arabia for a man and a woman to show any public display of affection (PDA), but its okay for two men to walk hand in hand, kiss, and even have sex. Luckily for me though, I never had to witness any male-on-male sex, but I saw plenty of kissing and interlocked pinkies on the bad streets of Dhahran.

Hell, on one occasion, I even saw a Saudi rug shop owner having oil rubbed into his body by five men from India, while he lounged in his chair. Since the last time I saw Bill and Hillary hugging and kissing on a beach, I can't remember a time I felt the need to puke at the mere sight of something. This chubby little Saudi man was so lazy that he simply snapped his fingers and another Indian came running from the back of the shop to ask me if I needed help in choosing a rug. What I really needed was a bucket to puke in.

What makes their actions even stranger is that although it is a common and even acceptable practice for men to engage in such activity, it is not acceptable when such activity involves love. So in this case, it is not the behavior that is abhorrent, it is the thought that offends Allah. Short of finding love letters, I'm not exactly sure how they can tell when love is involved. Maybe it's a twinkle in the eyes of the guilty parties that gives them away. I may not live in San Francisco or the Upper East Side, but as far as I'm concerned, a man would have to be pretty warped to think that holding another man's hand in public is okay, but doing the same with his wife or girlfriend is somehow an affront to God.

If you have ever served in the military, then you know that it is customary to be briefed on the customs and traditions of host countries you will be sent to. So, before my departure to Saudi, I and others were briefed. What we were told might shock you if you're a stupid American. Apparently, the definition of what it means to be a gentleman is a bit skewed. While stationed in Saudi, we were told that holding a door open for a woman could be considered an overt sexual act and that we should not do so. We were also told not to talk to women, look them in the eye or to physically assist them in any manner. Basically, you are not allowed to be gentleman in a Muslim country. I suppose all these stupid rules must have come about when some wise-ass Arab figured he was due a little-something for having assisted a lady in need of courtesy.

As far as punishment for any indiscretion of the mind or body is concerned, well let's just say logic and reason lost again. For instance, should any same-sex lovesick couple be discovered the penalties can range from several lashes to even death, depending on the severity of the love I suppose. Following this line of illogic, one might think that premarital sex between a man and a woman not in love would be okay, but it is not either. And, when it comes to punishment in heterosexual situations, it is generally the woman who will suffer the greatest retribution. Punishment for her is usually death, and while the family has the right to carry it out, should they get squeamish, they can always defer to the religious court. In some areas, it is even quite common for disgraced woman to be passed around and gang raped by men in her community. In many instances, the rape will often include some of the women's relatives.

Once she has been formally disgraced by the community in proper Islamic fashion, she is subsequently beheaded, stoned, stabbed or shot to death, and done so without even the slightest bit of hypocrisy. This form of Islamic justice (murder) is actually referred to as "honor killing." Even in cases where a woman has been raped, she is thought to have disgraced the family and expected to kill herself. With or without guilt women judged to have disgraced the family and Islam, can expect nothing short of a death sentence.

I suppose it never occurs to the rapists of these poor women that they are themselves guilty of premarital sex or adultery. Since, I've yet to find any shred of logic within Islam, I can't say that I'm entirely surprised. Hell, if murder doesn't bother them, why should a little thing like premarital or adulterous rape committed against a transgressor stand in the way? I don't mean to suggest that this goes on in the whole of Islam, but it is a well known fact that such brutality continues to this day unabated within every Muslim nation and even Western nations with Muslim populations. Personally, I don't really care how they justify their actions; if they really feel Allah has commanded them to do this, then Allah is most definitely not who they think he is. Quite frankly, I think these freaks have been so sexually repressed that they will take any opportunity to get a nut off, even if it means raping a defenseless woman condemned to death.

If all I've done is to confuse you further, let me summarize... First, it's okay for two men to have sex as long as they are not in love, but it's not okay for a man and a woman who are not in love to have sex. In the somewhat more logical world of the West, which do you suppose is seen as more troubling to the one true God? As for all you multiculturalists, hold on—there's more. It seems our peace-loving worldly neighbors are full of contradictions. Now, I don't necessarily mind when someone contradicts themselves; we've all been guilty of being inconsistent in our arguments or with the way we live our lives. But we're talking about an entire region of the world where, by my own estimation, a good 90 percent have chosen to drink the Kool-Aid.

Like many of our own spineless leaders, leaders in the Muslim world have to keep the Kool-Aid pitchers full in order to maintain the masses. They realize that without their daily serving of mass propaganda the collective could not be manipulated. What the Left and the spineless Right would like for us to believe, is that this is o.k. so long as our peace loving Muslim brothers can agree to disagree and keep it in their own backyard. If you're thinking of subscribing to this stupidity, you need to ask yourself if you really believe these freakazoids are going to crawl back into their caves and let the world pass them by.

The differences between our cultures extend way beyond whether society should have the right to beat the hell out of you or kill you for any indiscretion of the heart. Still, the West's argument shouldn't be how a transgressor of Islamic law should be punished for transgressions of the heart, but whether the transgressor should be punished at all for what is an individual's choice.

Many leftists in America may want to excuse radical Muslim behavior—much like our own criminals—by making excuses for their actions, but not knowing how to read or think for yourself is hardly an excuse for the savagery they have brought to the world. True, the propaganda machine in most Muslim countries is one that even Hitler's propaganda minister Joseph Goebbels could have admired, but so what? Did we excuse the Nazis and Japs for their evil actions? And, if they're saying that most Muslims are incapable of thinking for themselves, because they have been brainwashed, then are they not simply agreeing with me?

Well, I certainly believe that many are brainwashed, but I don't think our Muslim friends are buying any part of it. The truth is not something Muslims readily accept, especially when coming from an infidel. Whatever reason they use to excuse the inexcusable, few are as ridiculous as the claim by most Muslims that their society is superior to the West because of some ill-conceived belief that they are inherently virtuous by way of their faith. Still, I just love it when someone from the Islamic world claims superiority over the West, because it gives me another opportunity to show them for the dumbasses they are; especially when their claim of superiority is based solely on some idyllic view of Islam. And, I will prove that even virtue among Muslims is more about perception than reality.

Most Muslims refuse to accept the superiority of the West even when examples to the contrary are self-evident. You just have to wonder what is going on in their fragile little psyches every time they flip a light switch, drive a car, turn on a TV, flush a toilet, listen to recorded music, take modern medicine, operate a computer, or view a jet flying overhead. These are just a few of the everyday conveniences made possible by the West. And, their use of these modern inventions only illustrates their hypocrisy further. Do they not claim that the West and all things associated with it are evil? Well, if all that comes from the West is evil, does it not hold that the innovations of the West are evil too and if so, then why use them?

How virtuous can it be to use Western technologies? How virtuous is it to beg for money and food (Egypt, Sudan, Yemen, etc.) from the "Great Satan?" How virtuous is it to force someone to practice your religion? How virtuous is it to mutilate and torture people? How virtuous is it to murder people for something as simple as speaking their minds? How virtuous is it to control others' lives to your benefit? In the illogical world that is Islam, it is apparently virtuous to do all of these things. Do you still think that all cultures are equal?

Who do you suppose is the more virtuous man—the man who does the right thing of his own accord, or the man who does what is right only when he is told to? Of the two great religions and Islam, which do you suppose is more virtuous? Is it the Christian or Jew—who has a choice as to whether or not he will practice his faith and chooses to do so—or the Muslim, who has no choice and does so only because he is forced? Where exactly is the virtue in doing something that is presumed good only when you are forced to do it? Since the American Constitution and other Western societies recognize an individual's right to religious freedom, it should be apparent to you as to which is more virtuous.

The all-inclusive crowd in America love to tell us that it is our differences that make us strong. This is of course, a load of crap! What has made us strong, at least in the past, has been that most people immigrating to the U.S. adopted the American way of life. They may have clung to some simple aspects of their culture like food, music, and their native language, but I'll guarandamnteeyou they didn't bust their asses to get here so that they could bring oppression with them. Can you imagine what America would be like if every immigrant coming here was allowed to practice every aspect of their native culture? Would Medicare and HMOs then be required to pay for clitorectomies?

How about the Shiite sect of Islam? A common practice for every Shiite male each year is to flog himself about the forehead and back with whips and chains until he looks like he has just been mauled by a pack of pit bulls. This lovely religious ritual is to commemorate the bloody death of Mohammed's grandson, Hussein Ibn Ali. It has been noted that many men will lose up to a pint of blood during this lovely Islamic ritual and based on the fact that thousands fall or pass out on the streets every year it's practiced, it must be true. Now, if we could only get those pints up to quarts, say 3 to 4 quarts, the collective I.Q. of the world might increase substantially. But the true beauty of this religious ritual has got to be watching Shiite mothers beat their male toddlers and younger boys about the head and back until blood is drawn and all while the child screams in bloody terror.

Ah, I can see it now—soon some jackass ACLU attorney will be proclaiming a Shiite Muslim's right to march down every Main Street in America while he beats himself or his child about the head and back. It's all enough to give you that warm fuzzy feeling inside. Of course, after viewing such a spectacle you shouldn't feel like your American culture is superior either. As we all know, all cultures are equal, right?

I'll tell you what, if there is anything you should know about the Muslim world it's that the majority of Muslims have no intention of living in peace and harmony with the rest of us. If you haven't already, I would suggest that you un-cork your head from the orifice of your backside. You don't need to understand why they hate us, only that they do. If they had their way, we'd be stepping through doorways right foot first, wiping our butts with our left hands, and praying five times a day, and women wouldn't ever have to worry about getting sunburned again. Can you imagine a life in America where children no longer perform in plays, alcohol is banned, women are not allowed on the beach in bikinis, movies are censored, and walks in the park with your favorite gal are forbidden?

In America we still have freedom of choice, at least for now, and we still have the right to base our personal decisions on whatever criteria we find reasonable, without the intervention of the church or state. This doesn't mean that we will always take the right decision, but at least we reserve the right to screw up. Although many of America's politicians no longer defer to the Constitution when deciding on matters of law, the Constitution is still the supreme law of the land, and it still exists to protect the rights of each and every American.

It requires no logical stretch of the imagination to see that Islam, when practiced literally by its fanatics, is wholly incompatible with America on a cultural, philosophical, and economic basis. So, unless you're willing to give up everything that has made America great, I would suggest that you start speaking out against these lunatics—both leftists and terrorists alike. Personally, I enjoy girl-watching, outdoor barbecues, and praying when I choose to. I'm not about to give up those freedoms for a bunch of feminists who think girl-watching is sexist, or for some tree-hugging dumbass upset about my burning charcoal on the weekends, and that certainly goes for a bunch of Islamo-fascists upset about the frequency of my prayers and to whom they're directed.

The Left is so blinded by their multicultural stupidity, that they can't even see that it is they the Islamo-fascists hate most. What are they going to do when the Muslims come after them? Standing in unison while singing "We are the World" isn't much of a defense. Liberals need to realize that in the Muslim world humanity is still 1400 years behind and has no intention of catching up. They might also remember that there are no gay bars, environmental laws, women's rights, freedom of speech or religious freedoms in Islamic countries. In the Muslim world, a man can pour gas on a dog and set it ablaze just for kicks, and if you speak out against the Islamic state, you may just pay the ultimate price. But, if you still don't think you have anything to worry about or that the Muslim threat has been blown out of proportion, maybe the words of our enemies wake you up:

"We love death the U.S. loves life; that is the big difference between us." Osama bin Laden

Chapter 8
Judge Away

"A long habit of not thinking a thing wrong, gives it a superficial appearance of being right." Thomas Paine, in Common Sense

As any self-respecting Redneck will attest, true progress in life can only be made when people are willing to judge others for their actions. You see, without judgment, the lazy, stupid and otherwise useless might never be aware of their condition. Just how do you think Americans born in the early twentieth century became known as the "Greatest Generation?" Do you really think that it was because they were concerned about how others felt? Hell no they weren't concerned, and the reasons why should be obvious.

But, if they're not, you might start with the fact that they weren't raised by a bunch of non-judgmental politically-correct pantywaist leftists. And, as best as I can recall, the "Greatest

Generation" never had any compunction to judging others for their correctable failings. My Grandparents certainly never hesitated to call a spade a spade. If you were acting a fool or being a dumbass, not only were you going to hear about it, you were probably going to feel it too.

From the quick wit of Mark Twain on down to the folksy wisdom of Will Rogers, prior generations sure had many a fine example to quote when judgment was necessary. But even when another's wit and wisdom wasn't at the tip of their tongue, they were rarely at a loss to spin one of their own; whether as a metaphor or just straight-up. Unfortunately, their wit and wisdom is becoming more rare than a 18-year-old virgin on spring-break. Whatever the reason, whether its political-correctness or cultural equivocation, the fact is—our children are not getting the proper training necessary to prepare them for a life of casting dispersions on the shortcomings of their fellow man.

Never reticent to point out an individual's shortcomings when a trend in poor behavior presented itself, my Grandfather could spin a colloquial metaphor that would have made Mark Twain proud. While his and others abilities to wax eloquent on the useless probably stemmed from a life of hard work and a sense of earned pride, their capacity for observing and commenting on the obvious was a testament to their forthright character and backbone to call it like it is. Though sorely lacking in today's society, it was their observations and comments on the failed character of men that helped to make me the man I am today; a man undaunted by the stupidity of political-correctness and moral equivocation.

I can't tell you how I long to hear men and women of sound judgment describe the common-sense impaired with metaphors such as, "He ainta playin with a full deck!" or "That boys got shit fur brains!" Just as common and no less descriptive were those used to describe the lazy and useless. Ones like, "If breathing required effort, he'd be dead!" and "He's about as useless as tits on a warthog!" Still, not all were used to describe human failures. One of my personal favorites—often used to describe times when things were going generally well—was… "We must be shittin in high cotton!"

The idea of judging others for their actions, at least in a fundamental sense, that is, in a way that matters, almost never occurs anymore. Certainly not in a manner I had grown accustomed to. I'm sure you have heard some of these common remarks used to excuse stupidity; "Well, what are you going to do?" or "Kids will be kids!" or how about, "It's not his fault he was born that way!" The implication in each of these remarks is that the person responsible for the bad conduct is not to be held accountable. In essence, poor behavior has become expected of certain people and thus they must be given a pass.

As to why the pass is given, I've only been able to surmise that it is either out of sheer laziness or the horror many liberals must feel when judgment is necessary and subsequent action is required. Apparently the fear of judging and of being judged is a pathological trait for many liberals. For what might also be described as an identity crisis at best; liberals have developed a guilt complex for crimes and indiscretions they may or may not commit. I'm sure you have heard this one before, "I don't like to judge others; you never know when you might be in a similar situation!" Oh, I don't know… I'm pretty sure I'll never be a rapist, murderer, pedophile, wife-beater, junkie or dumbass. What more proof do you need of a weak and feeble mind than that of a liberal?

Liberals may think that by not passing judgment on their fellow citizens they are being just and fair, but they are not and for reasons that should be all too obvious. Just look around you, from the dumbasses of modern pop-culture to the little bastards racing up and down my street, this Nation is becoming increasingly disrespectful and it is a direct result of people refusing to judge the actions of others. If you don't think that an, "anything goes society" affects attitudes negatively, then I would ask you to go hang out at the mall, visit a public school or talk with a policeman.

For those of you who may be less daring, similar behavior can be heard whenever most politicians, Hollywood dumbasses or liberals of any sort open their mouths. If we continue to cower from our responsibility of judging others for their wrongful actions we shouldn't be surprised when all we get in return is more of the same. Remember that without judgment there can be no shame, without shame there can be no guilt and without guilt there may never be remorse. Ultimately, we'll be left with little more than a bunch of whiny little narcissistic shits thinking themselves deserving of all that they desire. Now, how can we expect our children to learn respect if they have no feelings of shame, guilt or remorse for their poor behavior?

The fact that more and more Americans are becoming disrespectful should be no secret to anyone and we sure as hell don't need another study to determine its cause and affect. The cause is the absence of judgment and the affect is a degenerate culture pushing us further into dissolution. America's lack of judgment is directly related to poor parenting, public institutions and a media full of degenerates. While much of the blame can be attributed to lazy, stupid and useless parents; Hollywood, public schools and the media in general are the primary culprits in perpetuating the myth that it is not right to judge others. The solution for poor behavior is simple and requires nothing less than verbal admonishment and possibly a sound whipping of Junior's ass. Restricting Junior from his connection to the outside world is useless. Such punishments require constant oversight and most parents almost always relent due to the constant whining and begging of their children.

Today, many parents are under the illusion that obedience and respect can be received if children are treated as equals. Some parents even go as far as to refer to their children as their best friends. I have only one thing to say to you knuckleheads... Grow up! You had your chance at childhood; now stop trying to relive it through your children. If you make them your equal you will never have their respect and I can guarantee you of one thing; they will take advantage of your weakness. Let's face it, Spock was an idiot and some children just need a swift kick-in-the-ass. With a little bit of ass-kicking I can guarantee you of another thing; they'll either shape up or ship out, either way problem solved. And, don't think that just because you refuse to judge and discipline your child, the real world won't. A dumbass can only go so far in life once un-tethered from the safety net of home.

Where the media is concerned, it would seem that they have acquired the unnatural power to hypnotize and/or brainwash large segments of the population. Understanding how this has occurred can be a bit complicated. Although, it would seem that the media and its hordes of politically correct morons have created a form of nationalistic peer pressure designed to misinform, under-educate and convert the weak-minded. This peer pressure has apparently caused millions of Americans to stop thinking for themselves and to give-up their good sense out of fear that they will be shunned should they show any sign of intolerance towards all things liberal and stupid.

Evidence of this can be seen daily as there is not a day that goes by in America that one isn't being bombarded with messages from Hollywood or other media outlets that homosexuality is perfectly normal, promiscuity in any situation is fine or that all cultures and people are of equal value. Should you happen to be one of the few Americans who think Hollywood is full of shit or who hasn't been scared into submission by your employer or a government institution, well... you're probably just a lawsuit away from being charged with a hate crime or forced into sensitivity training.

With increasing regularity far too many Americans are choosing to cast aside their core values and accept whatever stupidity is being thrown at them. This, my friends, is just plain un-American and we shouldn't stand for it. You should remember who you are and stop being a chicken-shit. Being a cowardly American is as unnatural as homosexuality. I say, "Screw the Left and all their utopian lunacy!" No American should ever be afraid to tell someone to, "Kiss my ass!" especially when that someone is trying to control your life and thoughts to their benefit.

If there were ever a time to cast dispersions or to make judgment calls it would be now. Think about it, who among us hasn't heard some yahoo, a close relative, friend or even a member of the church tell them, "Judge not lest ye be judged?" Their implication being that it's not your right to judge others. But this is bullshit, because they're only giving you half the story. What they hope you won't pay attention to, is the second part "... lest ye be judged?" Shouldn't the full translation of this statement be, "One should not judge others unless one is willing to be judged?" It does not say that one should not pass judgment, only that one should not pass judgment, unless one is willing to be judged. The very statement begs the question, so why the partial interpretation?

Now that you understand why so many fail to make judgments, it should be obvious why liberals only adhere to the "Judge not [...]" portion of this famous Biblical quote, that is, they want nothing to do with the second part, "lest ye be judged!" A full and complete translation would destroy everything they stand for. You see, once a judgment has been made, responsibility must be attached.

Think I'm wrong, well then, I have a homework assignment for you. Next time you're watching a liberal being interviewed and they're posed a question on how to deal with a particular issue, listen very closely. Regardless of the issue you will never hear them attach blame to their constituents or supporting collectives.

What I mean to say is that you will never hear a liberal say that a person is responsible for him or herself, it is contrary to their philosophy. Here is a typical liberal response with regard to the so-called plight of the poor:

Larry the Interviewer: Congressman, how do you think we should deal with the problems of the poor?

Liberal: Well Larry, I'll tell you, first we need to make sure that there are plenty of programs available to take care of them. Then we have got to get Republicans to go along with more funding. Without the funding of such programs we will not be able to take care of the poor.

Here is what a true Individualist or Conservative might say:

Conservative: You know Larry everyone is always asking; what should we do for the poor? Shouldn't we be asking what should the poor be doing for themselves? After all, I can't make them get off their ass and go to work, go to school or even to read a book that might better themselves. Instead Larry, why don't you tell me why you think I should punish the productive citizens of our Country for the misdeeds, laziness or stupidity of the poor and their enablers?

Liberals are always impressing upon us that people have a right to do as they please so long as it is within the bounds of the law. Though, even in matters of the law their sincerity is suspect. Still, what they will not say; is that people should accept responsibility for any negative result stemming from their actions. They can't, to do otherwise would be an admission that their ideology is a failed one and is fundamentally wrong.

Just ask yourself, would you readily pay your taxes if they told you that your confiscated wealth was going to people who refuse to work, not who could not work or to women who purposely get pregnant to receive state and federal (taxpayer) assistance or even to the homosexual who contracted AIDS after having sex with an average of 15 partners per year. By the way that statistic comes from the University of Chicago—hardly a bastion of conservative thought. If these self-repressed malcontents can approach their life with such indifference, why should others be expected to care? Because it's the moral thing to do, you say! Well, where in the hell were their morals? Besides, I thought we were not allowed to make moral judgments? What a bunch of stinking hypocrites!

Okay, let me put it another way. A liberal would never judge a bum to be lazy, a never-wed mother of several children to be a thoughtless welfare slut or a homosexual whore to be a deviant. To do so might cause two things to occur. First, liberals themselves might be subjected to judgment, something their self-esteem could not withstand. Second, responsibility would have to be assigned to the individual, not society. For instance, the man is a bum because he is lazy, the woman is a thoughtless slut because she will not keep her legs closed and has no regard for the life of her children and the homosexual is a deviant because he engages in unnatural acts with multiple partners and with no regard to his health.

You see, when the truth is revealed, responsibility must be attached. Liberals would like you to believe that cause and effect are mutually exclusive, but they are not. To put it, yet another way; a capable man who will not work is lazy, thus he is a bum. Now contrast this classical conservative definition with that of a liberal;

a capable man who will not work has not only society to blame, but its wealth to expect in exchange for a future vote.

Need more, well how 'bout this? If you believe you have a right to another's wealth without earning it, then I judge you to be wrong. If you believe you have a right to special treatment because of your sexual practices, or that America is great because of cultural differences among its citizens, then I judge you to be wrong. If you believe that an animal's life is of equal value to human life, or that you have the right to do as you please without suffering the consequences of your actions, then again I judge you to be wrong. Yes, the answers are obvious if not politically-correct and if we allow the Left to continue dismissing core American values as repressive ideas of the past, things will only get worse.

If you are still in need of additional clarity, then consider the following. Remember all those judgments your grandparents use to make about bums, unwed mothers, punks and those two strange men living together down the street in the corner house. Well, it seems that all those people had their wittle feelings hurt whenever someone chose to look the other way in disgust or to not condone their behavior by judging them for their poor conduct. Yes, when we get right down to it, this is all about certain people who have had their feelings hurt, at least those with low self-esteem who look to others for vindication of their actions.

But who in the hell ever said that one has a right not to have their feelings hurt, especially when faced with the truth. I know there are efforts underway to control free speech, but I'm not aware of any existing laws that prevent people from having their feelings hurt. Yes, there were and are laws against homosexual acts, but I'm only willing to accept your right to be gross and give me the heebee jeebies if you're willing to accept my right not to be forced to accept your lifestyle or to pay your medical bills when you get an STD as a result of your deviant behavior. Should you think that I'm being somewhat of a hypocrite, I hold the same standards for irresponsible conservative and liberal heterosexuals too.

Can you believe it? Because certain people within certain groups have had their wittle feelings hurt, a once great Nation of high moral character and standards has been reduced to a Nation of self-repressed whiny-ass little detractors. What a bunch of pansy-ass little girls. Well screw every last one of you little piss-ant cowards. If you want some respect, then at least be willing to accept the responsibility for your actions. If you did, I'd be one of the first to stand up in defense of your right to live as you please.

All of these whiners and nut-jobs need to understand that rational people judge others based on their actions and not how they feel. When you insist on defining who you are by your actions, don't be surprised when you are judged by the same. If you really desire the acceptance of others for whatever action defines you; then tell America that you are willing to accept the costs and consequences associated with them. Until then, do all sane and rational people a favor, either shut-up or go away.

While many of us are busy raising our families and living our lives, society's filthy, lazy and retched have been busy redefining the Nation's identity. By blurring the lines between what is right and what is wrong, they have succeeded in creating a society where absolutes no longer exist or that is at best, stuck in the middle. A life where no one is to be judged by their actions is exactly what they want from you. You may wish to call it a compromise, but I've yet to see how a society that tells you how and what to think for nothing in return is a compromise.

Besides, in a compromise between good and evil who do you suppose will be the real victor? Twenty years ago many homosexuals were saying that all they wanted was to be left alone and allowed to live their life as they choose, so a compromise was reached when most states abolished sodomy laws. Then the homosexual collective decided they wanted the same worker benefits afforded to married couples and a compromise was reached when some companies and States relented, even though benefits had never been afforded to unmarried heterosexual couples.

To the logical mind this would have meant that discrimination was based on marital status not sexual orientation. But, this did not matter. Later, homosexuals decided that the government should recognize same sex marriages, believing that full acceptance could be achieved if the definition of what it meant to be a family could be changed. Thus far only a few cities and states in America have compromised, albeit un-Constitutionally.

Now, homosexuals want laws created that specifically protect them against what they deem to be hateful speech and many States again have compromised by enacting Hate Crimes Legislation. In some areas under the so-called Hate Crimes Legislation it is now against the law to call a homosexual a fag or any other disparaging remark. So much for free speech! Ah, but wait there's still more; in addition to all prior compromises, the homosexual collective would also like the right to adopt children. I suppose no family is complete without two Dads or Moms that happen to sleep together. Since it is believed by some that children should only be adopted by parents of the same race, should anything happen to the homosexual parent(s) would we then be required to replace the prior homosexual parent(s) with new homosexual parent(s)?

Is it not enough to make these people happy that taxpayers are screwed out of countless billions to disproportionately fund AIDS research so that some politician may increase his odds of re-election? Personally, I would rather see my taxes go to the research of diseases that people have no control over. I can only imagine the pain a parent must feel to see their child suffer from a disease such as Muscular Dystrophy or Cancer, while knowing that the government was spending billions on a disease that could have been avoided in the first place with some self-control.

Now when two parties come to an agreement it is generally because each party has brought something to the table in exchange for something each had to offer. This is how most would define a compromise. In the prior paragraphs I used the word compromise only in jest, because no compromise ever occurred. What exactly was it that the homosexual community offered in all those so-called compromises? The only thing I would have asked for, was that they accept responsibility for their actions, but never once in all their demands did they ever make the offer.

If you are expecting an offer from the homosexual collective don't hold your breath. Should you ever ask whether they are willing to accept responsibility, don't expect a rational answer either. Oh, and for those of you who refuse to pass judgment or feign ignorance, before you think you're getting away with something; refusing judgment when it is the moral and right thing to do is also an act of evil. The German people tried that same excuse back in May of 1945, it didn't work then and it won't work in the future.

Chapter 9

Restrictive Shades of Brown

"A man receiving charity always hates his benefactor – it is a fixed characteristic of human nature." George Orwell

Before the Left redefined multiculturalism as a political movement—a movement whose only goal is to subjugate American culture to lesser and foreign cultures—it was simply a term used to describe how one might relate or adapt to other cultures. Still, it was probably for its somewhat innocuous and original meaning that the Left even chose the word as a way to help disguise their true intent. With its all-inclusive undertones, the Left must have thought they would be safe labeling their newest anti-American movement as "multiculturalism." After all, if anyone were to ever object or challenge their intentions, all they would have to do is quote the original definition and yell "racism!"

But, as usual, they failed to realize that actions mean more than words. Because, contrary to their stated claim of only wanting to bring cultures together, it is evident by their actions that their only intention was to propagate a delusional perception that America attained its greatness not through philosophical commonality, but through cultural diversity. But since I do not worship at the altar of political-correctness or accept the idiotic adage that, "Perception is Reality" I'll tell it to you like it really is.

Merriam-Webster defines "multiculturalism" as, "relating to, reflecting of... or adapted to diverse cultures." Well, relate as I may and reflect as I have, there isn't a snowball's chance in hell that I will ever adapt to another culture, much less respect any philosophy or economic system that does not recognize the individual rights of men. Taking such a position is really quite easy once you realize and accept why American culture is superior to all others. Just how inferior another culture is usually depends on how collectivized or controlling their governments are.

Certainly, some cultures suck less than others and some liberals may be lesser dumbasses than others, but that doesn't mean I have to accept the lesser of two or more evils. Too simplistic! Well, how about this? Any culture or philosophy that forces individuals to accept its tenets is evil. Just how successful do you think a collectivist system such as; fascism, socialism or communism would be if its citizens weren't forced to participate. For this reason alone, the superiority of capitalism or of an individualist culture should be obvious as neither requires the forced acceptance of others to be viable.

Given the Left's manipulation and outright bastardization of the true meaning of multiculturalism, it's easy to see how Webster's definition falls short in the context of today's political environment. To understand why multiculturalism is portrayed in a positive, albeit restrictive manner, you need only observe the cultural collectivization of specific groups as it relates to the Left's agenda. Still, how one feels about the word and the intent of its use generally depends on their view of America. If you have yet to form an opinion due to a lack of understanding, the following should help you to come to your own conclusion by way of my sheer common-sense.

Yes, at first glance the word multiculturalism does appear to be an innocuous term, engendering neither good nor bad thoughts. The word even appears to define itself. As a result— less any preconceived notions—one might be inclined to define the word as; a system whereby all cultures are included. Some may envision it to mean; a multitude of cultures living within a shared geographical area. Others might imagine; a collective utopia where many cultures live in peace and harmony with one another. Still, others might instantly reject it for the load of crap it has become. You can count me as one of the latter.

These three words might also help you to understand how I really feel—Multiculturalism my ass! First of all, there is nothing inclusive or legitimate about the disaffected montage of loons promoting this crap. I've never once been invited to a Black, Hispanic, Muslim, Queer, Communist, Socialist, Anarchist or Pro-death meeting, gathering or protest of any sort. Except for self-effacing white liberals, I have never seen, read nor heard of any Whites (Of the conservative persuasion), Capitalists or Pro-life groups being included in any multicultural rally, demonstration, gathering or meeting of any sort either. As all leftist propaganda does, it purports one thing and does another.

For those taking the Conservative point-of-view, I say we call and define the multicultural movement as it really is. Thus, multiculturalism as practiced by the Left, shall be known henceforth by its new and more proper name, "Ethnocentric Collectivism" and defined as such:

1. A doctrinal belief by minority groups and various sub-cultures that individualism, capitalism and the idea of personal responsibility are evil constructs of Western societies.
2. An aggregation of cultures whose skin pigmentation falls within an acceptable range of brown (i.e., Restrictive Shades of Brown).
3. A system whereby its adherents only accept those who believe in a communal, progressive, socialist or communist State.

For those of you who may have similar opinions towards multiculturalism and who have stated them publicly, I don't have to tell you how swift condemnation from its proponents can be. Charges of hate, prejudice and racism can fall down on you faster than a liberal running from the truth. But what else can you expect from those whose arguments have no basis in reality? When you have no argument, your only options are to either walk away or remain and show your stupidity.

The claim by ethnocentrists (multiculturalists) that it is not possible for Americans to share a common culture is just one of their many stupid arguments. Assuming that Americans are incapable of having in their culture, a common thread or philosophy which binds them, requires a total disconnect from the reality that there is a difference between how someone lives their life culturally and philosophically. What their distorted little minds prevent them from understanding, is that there is a greater cultural philosophy that exists and that it is this philosophy that brings most Americans together.

Just how to explain this I thought would be a bit tricky, but once I got to thinking again, I discovered it's really quite simple. After all, I have already alluded to it several times, which is, that many Americans choose to make a distinction between their *cultural lifestyle* and their *cultural philosophy*. The difference between the two is that it is our cultural philosophy that unites most of us and our culture lifestyle that identifies us. It is our cultural philosophy that has at its foundation the American idea of, "Life, Liberty and the Pursuit of Happiness." Our cultural lifestyle is what separates us into groups defined by such things as; race, religion, language, food, music, dress and other customs. Yes, America is filled with an array of ethnicities and races, but this does not mean that our strength lies within such diversity.

Hitler, a socialist and new-age earth worshipping pagan dumbass of his day took the same fallacious position as many liberals do today. In fact, during WW II, both Germany and Japan believed most inaccurately that a Nation of immigrants from numerous countries could never find common ground, much less unite to fight a war on the scale they would unleash on the world. While we now know just how wrong they were, my point is that no matter how different we were, when the shit-hit-the-fan we united to defend a single philosophy. Of course, if the "Amnesty for Illegals" crowd gets its way and ethnocentrists continue to subvert America's philosophical culture, I'm not so sure what we'll fight for in the future. Hmm, you'd think that that's just what they want.

As you learned from Chapter 3's "The ist Factor", their intentions are no accident. If they were to ever acknowledge the existence of a distinct American culture or philosophy, they would have to admit to the American people that they are against it. Even in current-day America, such an admission would mean their ultimate demise. By refusing to admit that a distinct

American culture exists, the Left is able to deny historical fact and spread their anti-American propaganda.

They will never accept that American culture is defined by a philosophy of individualism, as they have rightly concluded that thinking and self-reliant individuals have no need of the State and therefore of them. Their entire existence is predicated on the collectivization of individuals with complaints about how their group isn't being served; never asking whether they should be served in the first place and if so, by whom?

Don't get me wrong, I have no problem with individuals seeking cultural division for the sake of comfort, community and commonality. Because in a free society, the one "C" word that brings us all together is capitalism. But, when the State anoints itself the purveyor of goodwill by purposely supporting government defined groups over the rights of individuals they have overstepped their bounds. In the end, the only thing they have been successful at doing with their false charges of greed, racism and sexism is pitting the desires of government sanctioned groups against the rights of individual Americans.

The grouping and sometimes forced collectivization of certain people doesn't just hurt those who are forced to support it, it also creates a group-think mentality for current and subsequent generations to follow, as prior generations tend to stifle any independent thought among the subsequent generations. This is readily apparent among the welfare class as second, third and even forth generations are doing as their predecessors have done before them; that is, sitting on their ass and collecting a check while complaining about those who are forced to be their benefactors.

With rare exception every race, ethnicity and culture that has come to America has segregated itself. When thousands of

Irish came to America in the mid to late 1800s they didn't rejoice in their differences with Americans of English, Scottish, French or German ancestry. When hundreds of thousands of Italians came in the early 1900s they didn't celebrate their differences with the Irish, English, Scottish or Germans either. In just about any city one might have visited in America you would have found Italians living in predominantly Italian neighborhoods and the same would have been true for the Irish, Germans, English, Russians, Scottish, Pols and Czechs.

People simply chose to live in those areas where they could find commonality. Although immigrants of yore sought comfort among their own, they not only came to identify themselves as real Americans, but had to pass a battery of verbal, written and physical tests for the honor to do so. Today, most immigrants, both illegal and legal still gather in like communities, but few have any intention of ever identifying themselves as real Americans and only complain when asked to learn the language or pass a physical. Maybe when it comes time to receive a check or when its time to vote for another P.O.S. to steal on their behalf they'll smile real big and wave the American flag, but not as true Americans. What multiculturalism has taught them is that their cultural philosophy is of equal value and somehow worth maintaining.

Though I do not think it anyone's business to unite us, I find it odd that those who promote cultural acceptance also support the idea that race and ethnicity are the only legitimate means for individuals to find commonality. Who among us hasn't heard the claim that only Blacks can represent Blacks or that only Mexicans and now Asians can represent their respective race? Need additional proof? Next time a Black, Hispanic or Asian accomplishes something of significance observe their respective community—what you are likely to see is local and national minority leaders touting their individual achievement as the collective achievement of their race. Conversely, these same idiots will blame Whitey for whatever failures are prevalent among their race. What they are in essence saying is... that Whitey is collectively responsible for all that ails their community and that they are collectively responsible for all that is good in their community.

Why do you suppose it is that neither achievement nor failure is attributed to the individual among the various minority cultures in America? When a white man discovered a vaccine for polio, invented the personal computer and broke the DNA code, did Eisenhower, Reagan or Bush claim these as the achievements of white culture? Did whites gather en masse to claim superiority over all others? No, they did not. I would hope that they did not because these were not the accomplishments of a collective group of white people; they were the accomplishments of individuals.

If I were a black man and had accomplished something of great importance only to have poverty pimps like Jesse Jackson, Al Sharpton or Sheila Jackson Lee step forward to ascribe credit to their efforts, I would be pissed off. Still, if credit must be given to any group, I say it does belong to Whitey. After all, it was Whitey that wrote this Nation's founding documents and it was Whitey that wrote the Civil Rights Act of 1964. Let's not also forget that it is Whitey who pays the majority of the tax bill in this country.

How is it, that Whitey can be blamed for all that is wrong in the minority community, but can't be given any credit for its accomplishments? Is it logical to assume that Whitey is omnipotent only in the realm of evil? If liberals define 'good' by how much one is allowed to take from another, then shouldn't Whitey be considered the epitome of 'good' and the most virtuous race on this planet? Is it not Whitey that has allowed the wanton of society to take a great amount of his wealth? In the liberal's finite view of the world, does he not claim that Whitey controls nearly all wealth?

Really now, if it is your contention that you need preferential treatment and/or a government program in order to be successful, you are making the statement that Whitey holds your destiny in his hands. I know others pay taxes, but who is it in general that pays the majority of taxes in America and what group do you suppose it is that contributes the most in the creation and funding of all those wonderfully unsuccessful social programs? Whether you like it or not, the answer is Whitey and if you have taken advantage of any taxpayer funded program, you have mostly Whitey to thank. Every time you vote for a politician that promises you more of another's wealth you have taken the position that you are incapable of providing it for yourself and are in need of Whitey's help.

It simply must be so, because according to the IRS, nearly 97% of all taxes are paid by the top 50% of wage earners. If Whitey makes up approximately 70% of the population, and possesses the majority of wealth, as liberals contend, then Whitey must be responsible for paying the majority of taxes collected by our government at all levels. Tell me, is it not these taxes that pay for all those social programs? Greedy my ass, as far as I can tell the only greedy ones are those on tax-payer assistance who keep demanding more and offer nothing in return.

A Follow on:

If all this makes you uneasy, don't despair. With a little bit of knowledge and fortitude you can take on the anti-American as well. Still, you will need to be prepared for all that they are likely to throw at you. Accusations of prejudice or of being a Nazi, bigot, racist, or homophobe will come at you faster than Chinese money at a Democratic Candidate. But do not be intimidated, because with all things illogical they can be easily deflected with the facts. For those who are not convinced, before you call me a bigot or tell me that I am stereotyping people, you need to have a basic understanding of statistics as it relates to generalizations.

For instance, a generalization can be made when statistically speaking, a certain outcome/result is to be expected. Whether we are talking about people, places or things doesn't matter either. For instance, if I were to place ten balls in a bag, six of which are red and four of which are blue and asked you to take one from the bag, there would be a 60 % chance that you would take a red ball. Correct?

So, using this same logic, might I also generalize the political leanings of a particular race, religion or ethnicity when the majorities of each have proven to have similar views. For instance, if I have determined that Islamic nations are a dangerous place for Jews and Christians to visit based on Muslim actions towards both, might I logically conclude that most Muslims find me unfit to live out my days as a Christian.

Since I am also no fan of fascism, socialism, or communism might I also generalize that countries like Cuba, Venezuela, China, Russia or North Korea are not in my best interests either. Sure, I might like a particular country's food, scenery, art or even the way the women dance, but that doesn't make them morally acceptable or America's philosophical equal.

Though I find America to be inferior to none, there are many sub-cultures in America that I also choose not to be a part of. My choice has nothing to do with race, ethnicity or whether you're a lawyer either, but everything to do with commonality. The fact that I haven't many Black, Hispanic or Asian friends, is only due to the fact that I have yet to meet many with similar views. But, the same goes for white people. I'm no more likely to contribute to the ACLU than I am to the NAACP or LULAC. I would love for all Americans to think of their country as I do, but they don't. What truly matters to me, is that we share a philosophy that does not impinge on one another's life.

The fact is, I don't like to hang around with anyone I don't have anything of value in common with—it's boring. What would be the point? The only time I have ever enjoyed myself with someone I had nothing in common with, was when I was with the opposite sex and we were engaged in things other than political dialog or who builds the best truck. Sure I'm civil and I interact with many different people on a daily basis never knowing where they stand philosophically. I may have my suspicions based on generalizations (statistically speaking), but I don't let it get in the way of being a civil and rational human being.

For many of the same reasons that I do not spend time with those of a particular race, religion or ethnicity I do not hang out with radical environmentalists, feminists, socialists, communists or militant homosexuals. Politically, culturally and philosophically I rarely have anything in common with these folks. Why would I want to hang out with a bunch of anti-Americans? Try as they may to convince me otherwise, there is nothing American about basing your very existence on whether others can be forced to agree, accept or provide for you.

Chapter 10
Mexitinians

"Only a virtuous people are capable of freedom. As nations become corrupt and vicious, they have more need of masters." Benjamin Franklin

If recent protests in several American cities by illegal aliens—mostly from Mexico—tell us anything, it's that most have no more intention of assimilating into American society than do most Muslims to the modern world. No matter how hard their multiculturalist proponents try to convince true Americans otherwise, it's obvious by their actions that they no more give a rat's ass about America and its true culture, than an Islamist cares about other religions.

If you have doubts as to the Left's complicity in the organization of these protests for the benefit of illegal aliens, you might try showing up at one so that you can witness first-hand their anti-American agenda. The envy, hate and stupidity exhibited by the illegal immigrant and others are so obvious that there can be no question in the mind of the observer as to their agenda. I urge you to go to one of these anti-American events and see for yourself who it is that's the driving force behind these protests.

Illegal immigrants and their supporters should remember that it was their choice to come here. They left their country for a reason; surely it was not to bring the failures of their culture with them? If their culture was truly better, then why leave it? Whether immigrants come legally or illegally are they not in affect, admitting to the superiority of American culture? It would serve immigrants well to remember why it was that they left their country in the first place. Chances are, whatever the reason was, we don't want it here.

To add insult to our unwanted tax burden, it's not uncommon to see many of today's immigrants waving the flags of their country of origin as though they are some source of pride. Hardly a day goes by that I don't see the flags of many third world nations plastered on cars, waving from antennas, printed on T-shirts and even waving in front of homes. Where does this national pride come from? What great thing(s) have happened in these cesspools to make their citizens so proud that they would want to leave and come to America to show us their stupid flag? I always thought pride came from having actually accomplished something.

Immigrants may have once come to America to escape poverty and oppression, but today it seems that most only want to show us how proud they are of their country. Of all the American history I've ever read or heard of prior to the 1960s, I can't recall a single immigrant group that ever demanded so much for nothing. Just how many Hungarian, Russian, German, Italian, Japanese, Chinese or Spanish (citizens of Spain) groups do you know of that demand they be given free transportation, medical care, or housing? How many do you also know of that demand their children be taught in their native language? And just how many other countries are you aware of that are actively engaged in changing our laws to let millions of their citizens come into our country illegally?

The situation is only getting worse with multiculturalism constantly reinforcing the inaccurate idea that immigrants can maintain their philosophical culture in America and that becoming a citizen doesn't mean becoming an American. Because of multiculturalism (liberal speak for segregation) we are no longer a melting-pot; we are a pressure cooker whose legitimate culture has reached its boiling point and if we don't turn off the flame of illegal immigration soon, it will explode.

It just doesn't make sense why an immigrant, illegal or otherwise, would risk their life in some cases to flee a country that has shit on them, just to recreate it here. Don't get me wrong, the problem with most illegals isn't that they are Mexican; it's that they don't want to come here legally and once here try to become Americans; they want America to become Mexico. They want all the benefits America has to offer, but at Mexican prices. Unless of course, Whitey is paying for it and then, who cares what it costs?

America isn't the only place where illegal and unchecked legal immigration is causing a problem. Similar occurrences of what is happening to America can be seen all over the industrialized world. Other countries such as Germany, France (who cares) and Israel are also having issues with vastly different cultures threatening their own. The cost of illegal immigration in all these places is also far more than is received in tax revenue from the same source. Since the majority of American politicians are too cowardly to come up with new and innovative ways of dealing with the problem of illegal immigration I got to thinking again and came up with an idea I feel whose time is long since due.

To offset the burden being placed on our citizens by illegal aliens, I propose that we bill the illegal alien's country of origin for all costs associated with their care. I know, I know, you're thinking they'll never pay it. Well, if they refuse, we should cut off any loans, IMF funding and/or trade, something I am sure most could ill afford. What they will then be forced to do is control their population and borders. Since many of these immigrants arrive illegally and in many cases are assisted by their government, this solution would appear to be completely fair and logical.

Next to sealing off our borders with the military, I see this as the only other alternative for dealing with the problem in a responsible manner. Unless we start to exert some pressure on nations who export their problems, they will continue to take advantage of our welfare state and we can ill afford the debt illegal immigration places on our Nation. To expect American citizens to shoulder the burden of the world's poor is not only immoral, but a threat to American culture and a great burden on our economy.

Though examples are many, we'll take a cursory look at a few other nations and dig a little deeper into our own. Take Israel, a country surrounded by several Islamic states hell-bent on destroying them for nothing other than being Jewish. Israel once allowed hundreds of thousands of these same people to cross freely into their country to fill a labor shortage. As envy grew and terrorism and tension increased, Israel had to erect a wall not just to stop fanatical homicide bombers, but also to stem illegal immigration. Somehow Palestinian Arabs began to misconstrue their privilege to work in Israel with that of nationhood.

As many Mexicans have proclaimed a desire for the same, as it relates to the Southwest portion of the United States, we had better take notice and consider our advice to Israel more carefully. The price of peace has never been appeasement. If such acts, as perpetrated by the Palestinians, were to be carried out by Mexicans, I've no doubt that we would not stand for it. So what gives us the right to ask Israel to take crap from Palestinians and other crazy Islamists? Israel should push the Palestinians into Jordan and/or the Sinai Desert and give them one ultimatum... cease and desist immediately or you will be destroyed!

Okay, that explains Israel and as for Europe, well I really don't care, but why us? When you consider that an overwhelming majority of Americans want the borders sealed and illegals sent home packing you have to wonder. While you would expect foreign forces to be working against American interests, you might be surprised to know that it is mostly American politicians and businessman serving their own interests that allows illegal immigration to continue undeterred.

Faced with a shrinking base, Democrats court both the legal and illegal immigrants in the same manner as their domestic base, with a promise of freebies paid for by others in exchange for a vote. The Republicans, not to be out done, have jumped on board with many of the same promises and with the added benefit of providing cheap labor for big business, at least for those who know where to send their campaign contributions. Although illegal immigrant labor is cheap for big business, it's the American taxpayer who pays for their benefits package, yet this doesn't seem to bother either Party.

What some Republican leaders are either blind to or too stupid to figure out is that in the end it is they who will lose. Because, even if Amnesty is passed by a Republican Administration, there's little chance illegal immigrants will return the favor with a majority of their votes. With Democrats promising them more of America's wealth with no conditions attached, they have no incentive to assimilate or accept responsibility for themselves.

Aside from the internal forces unduly influencing our Nation's immigration policy, there are others the government and liberal media outlets don't want most Americans to know about. Afraid that their actions might incite an even greater uproar among the legitimate citizenry of America; the words and actions of these Mexican radicals are muted in the public arena so as not to sway American public opinion further against Amnesty. These Mexican radicals are not only insisting on things such as amnesty and unearned benefits, but often suggest that America's southwest region (from California to Texas) be ceded to Mexico.

Think I'm full of it or that what is happening in Israel could never happen here? Then check out some of these quotes from so-called Mexican-Americans and Mexican Nationals:

Richard Alatorre (Los Angeles City Council) – "They're afraid we're going to take over the government institutions and other institutions. They're right. We will take them over… We are here to stay."

Professor Jose Angel Gutierrez (University of Texas) – "We have an aging white America. They are not making babies. They are dying. The explosion is in our population… I love it. They are shitting their pants with fear. I love it."

Jose Pescador Osuna (Mexican Consul General) — "We are practicing 'La Reconquista' in California."

Augustin Cebada (Brown Berets) — "Go back to Boston! Go back to Plymouth Rock, Pilgrims! Get Out! We are the future. You are old and tired. Go on. We have beaten you. Leave like beaten rats, you old white people! It is your duty to die... Through love of having children, we are going to take over."

Should you require more evidence visit the web sites of La Raza, LULAC, MALDEF and MEChA just to name a few. Much like the uneducated brainwashed Palestinian, the Mexitinian thinks he can over populate a region, like the rat infested crumbling infrastructure of Mexico, and destroy it from within. If the Mexican fantasy to occupy Southwest America were to be realized, what do you suppose they would replace the existing government with?

Since, it is obvious they cannot provide for or govern themselves in Mexico, what makes them think they will be able to govern themselves north of the border. Would they even keep the same constitutional form of government? To keep the same form of government would be an admission that Whitey's form of government is in fact superior. Not to mention that it would have been Whitey's form of government that allowed them to come to power in the first place.

You can see how this would contradict their entire ethnocentric propaganda. If something so good can be shown to come from Whitey, then it might be more difficult to prove Whitey entirely evil. Let's imagine for just a moment that Whitey decided to pack his bags and leave the region of the Southwest, and upon his departure the new inhabitants took over and declared the end of Whitey and his Constitution. What do you think would happen next? I have no doubt that within a matter of a few years the Southwest region after being pilfered and plundered would be reduced to an image of modern day Mexico.

So absorbed by his unearned pride the Mexitinian has rendered himself completely incapable of seeing that it has been our particular form of government that has allowed us to become the prosperous Nation he so envies and despises. The Mexitinian appears to be unaware of the fact that if Americans were to be pushed out, no one would exist to fund the welfare state he requires to exist. They are bigger fools than even I believe if they think that it is possible to replace capitalism with a corrupt socialist meritocracy? When the U.S. Constitution no longer exists; what unalienable rights of the people will they recognize? Will drug dealing become the number two industry in the Southwest territories, second only to the oil industry, which would surely be nationalized within a matter of days by a new corrupt Mexican government?

Since, it is obvious that many Mexitinians do not know their own history, the following education has been provided. First of all, the Southwest region of America they lay claim to is not their ancestral homeland. That distinction belongs to the many American Indian tribes (Apache, Comanche, Pueblo, etc...) of the Southwestern portion of what is now: California, Arizona, New Mexico and Texas. In fact, the Mexican race is one of the newest races in the history of all Mankind. Another, though slightly newer race would be the Filipinos. Both Mexicans, a Central American Indian Spanish mix and Filipinos, an Asian Spanish mix owe their existence in part to the Spanish.

While the Spanish were out and about conquering new lands in the 1500s, 1600s and 1700s they brought with them diseases that the various tribes of Central America and the Philippines had no natural defenses against. Diseases brought by the Spanish like small pox and syphilis decimated entire regions. It has been noted by several anthropologists that up to 97% of Aztecs and other indigenous peoples were destroyed, not by war, but rather by disease alone. Since the Spanish decided to stay a while in the areas they had conquered they naturally commingled with the indigenous population. This was a good thing for their future offspring as immunity to certain diseases had developed.

So, if Mexicans must hate someone, shouldn't it be the Spanish? But, since Spain was never able to amass the great fortunes that America has earned and since Mexico has no real Navy to speak of, Spain should be safe for now. Mexico will just have to be happy with blaming America for its failures. Still, you would think that by osmosis alone, due to Mexico's proximity to the wealthiest Nation in the world that Mexico and even South American countries could emulate, at least a small portion of the success attained by the United States.

But no, just like the Middle East, most of Africa and portions of Southeast Asia, they remain third world nations comprised of two dominant classes; the very poor and the very rich. The poor is dominant in population and the wealthy by its power. With all the advancements that have taken place in the world, it is amazing that this continues to be the case, even though the ruling classes of these countries generally make up, on average, less than 5% of the population.

You would think that the remaining 95% could learn something from our history. So, just in case something was lost in translation, I spell it out slowly... it's called a R E V O L U T I O N! Sure you have had them in the past, but they were always for the wrong cause. Communism is not a legitimate cause, it's a curse and Fidel Castro, Che Guevara and Hugo Chavez are no leaders. They were and are all cowards. Really, we don't mind if you copy our Constitution, in fact, we would consider it an honor. Hell, we might even chip in. We have always been for the underdog in the cause of justice. Given our own humble beginnings you can understand why it is in our nature to help those in search of justice and freedom.

Surely you Mexitinians know by now, that in the history of the world, the U.S. is the only one that has come close to getting it right. Your desire to be here should prove that. The reason for your admiration and envy is our success, but don't be discouraged, because you can do it too. If you're still wondering how we did it, stop wasting your time and read our Constitution, then demand the same from your government. If they will not accept your demands then you will have to fight for them. It really is that simple. Stop blaming others and playing the "Woe is me game" and get off your ass.

Something should also be said to all you Mexitinians who whine about the United States while you plot and scheme in ways to steal from her. I understand that you are in the unenviable position of being a loser. I have heard all your bravado and it is as weak as your character. Why don't you stop talking and try to take her? I'll tell you why, because without her you would have no-one to steal from if you did. Do you really think that you can attain what we have as a Nation without our form of governance? Are you stupid enough to think that by emulating Mexico, Europe or some other worthless socialist state that you will somehow be able to prosper?

Please, do us all a favor and just shut up! You know as well as I, that should you ever attempt to take that which was never yours to begin with, you will be smacked down. The Treaty of Guadalupe-Hidalgo signed in 1848 was not a usurpation of land from Mexico by the United States. The Treaty was Mexico's way of stopping Manifest Destiny from moving South. History should have taught you what just a few Texans are capable of doing even when faced with overwhelming odds. REMEMBER THE ALAMO!

It doesn't matter if you out number us 10,000 to 1, you will be defeated. Should you ever attempt anything as silly as that which you propose, you will find yourself once again groveling at our feet. Only next time it may be from south of the Panama Canal. If you have to be angry about something, be angry that we decided to stop at the Rio Grande and not the Panama Canal.

Chapter 11

Aint Logic a Bitch!

"Government's view of the economy could be summed up in a few short phrases: If it moves, tax it. If it keeps moving, regulate it. And if it stops moving, subsidize it." Ronald Reagan

Though this book has been much ado about liberals and their collective worship of the secular State, I am not so naïve as to think that they are the only ones responsible for selling-out America to special interests. Many so-called conservatives, otherwise known as, neo-cons have proven themselves equally adept at screwing the country for personal gain. While the Left's sellout is much more apparent, due to their outward displays of anti-Americanism; neo-cons have preferred a more subtle approach. These so-called agents of free-trade and open-markets have sold-out and continue to sellout America to both corporate and foreign interests for their own benefit.

Yes, many differences may still exist between liberals and true conservatives, but few exist between liberals and neo-conservatives. Of those that remain, let's just say a Muslim thief would have no problem counting them on one hand. As proof, I need only remind you of the multi-billion dollar boondoggle to add drug benefits to Medicare for the elderly. The creation and passage of this legislation was due entirely to neo-con efforts. Mark my words; today it's the elderly getting a free-ride, tomorrow it will be the children, then the poor, only to be followed by the rest of us. The spreading of this socialist bureaucracy won't stop at demographics either, as liberals and neo-cons alike will seek to expand coverage to other medical services. Before we know it, the federal government will have completely back-doored the entire Nation into socialized medicine.

Now consider that neo-cons are attempting to grant amnesty to millions of illegal aliens for the benefit of big business and that Bush and friends approved of and lobbied for the sale of U.S. Ports to Dubai, an Islamic country known to support and sympathize with terrorists. Are these people nuts? While the prospect of Hillary Clinton, Barack Hussein Obama or any other leftist nut having power is scary enough, neo-cons have done little to prove that they are any different. Under their control, the size of government and the number of bureaucratic minions pouring over every facet of our lives has grown substantially. Where once we might have expected Republicans to counter attacks by Democrats on liberty and capitalism, the neo-con element has been virtually non-existent, and appears to have all but removed the Republican Party from the fight.

Since the neo-cons hijacking of the Republican Party, rarely do we ever see Republican leaders leading the charge in any economic or cultural battles against their once arch nemesis. By all accounts, their only contention with the Left seems to be with who can enact the next piece of socialist legislation in order to sway public opinion in their favor. Both sides have become so vacuous and deficient in all manner of logic and reason that without prior knowledge of either, one would be hard pressed to know who stands for what. Certainly neither side has proven to be on the side of the Constitution.

Seeing how the neo-cons have determined that the only way to defeat the Democrats is to restructure the Republican Party in their likeness, the American people appear to be left with only two illicit choices: 1) communist-light or 2) compassionate-socialism. On just about every controversial issue, neo-cons have ceded to the Left for fear that their propaganda wing—the mainstream press, will vilify them. Instead of taking their fight to the streets and trusting in the American people, they cower before the untrue spoken and written words of an anti-American leftist press. While fears of not being re-elected have caused many to compromise and even adopt liberal views, few if any seem to even care how their, "policy of containment" is actually aiding in the destruction of American culture and even the eventual demise of their own Party.

While the Left has done nothing to quell the ranting and raving of the lunatics on their side, neo-cons appear unable to mutter even the slightest protest for fear that they may be labeled insensitive. They seem to have been duped into believing that Americans are tired of negative campaigning and thus should play nice. If this were true, then why do liberals continue to assail conservatives with their nonsensical arguments and petty name calling? Americans are not tired of negative campaigning; they are tired of politicians who lack backbone and who shun American ideals. What I and millions of other real conservatives are tired of, is a bunch of spineless pantywaist Republicans who will not fight for what is right.

Neo-cons were so convinced by the press that Americans were tired of the arguing and negative campaigning that they went so far as to re-package the conservative movement and brand it with their own moniker. Unfortunately, their new brand of politically-correct conservatism—otherwise known as compassionate conservatism—didn't stop with the name change, as it wasn't long after the name change that compassionate-conservatism would become synonymous with compromise. From that moment on, neo-cons were off to the Treasury, as compromise after compromise occurred on issues such as: campaign finance reform, social programs, education and Supreme Court Justices.

Bush and his neo-con buddies have ceded so much precious ground to the Democrats that the only thing they can claim to have accomplished is the reshaping of the Republican Party in the Left's likeness. Why neo-cons felt a change was necessary, I'm not exactly sure. Other than a bunch of whinny-ass liberals complaining about how insensitive they were, I never felt there was ever a political Party more compassionate than the Republicans. So, if I could make one suggestion to the "newspeak" crowd of the Republican Party, I would suggest that if ya'll are feeling guilty about those things conservatives are suppose to stand for, then change sides and use your money to apologize. That which I have earned is not yours to take to assuage any feelings of guilt you may have.

Personally, I have nothing to apologize for; it is the neo-cons who should apologize to every true conservative for having made their Party in the likeness of the Democratic Party. Without a legitimate counter to the Left, the neo-con brand of conservatism guarantees us of only one thing, the certain death of liberty. Whether it's the eminent death of liberty offered by liberals or the slow methodical death offered by conciliatory neo-cons, I'm not willing to accept either. I make no apologies for being an Individualist or a Capitalist. Instead, I say to all those who would have me suffer at their indulgence to; "Kiss my white American ass!" When it comes to "Life, Liberty and the Pursuit of Happiness" I compromise with no one.

Is this not exactly what our Forefathers told the King of England? I know they did it much more eloquently than I could ever hope to, but I've no doubt that upon receipt of "The Declaration of Independence" King George must have turned to his Royal suck-ups and said, "They just told me to kiss their ass!" Our Forefathers understood that for any system of governance to be successful, it would have to be built on a moral foundation. They also knew that before the foundation of this new system could ever solidify, the rights of men would have to be unalienable, that is, of God. What this meant, was a total dissolution of all ties which bound them to the monarchy or to others who might try to limit their liberty.

It was they who first recognized, accepted and then enacted a Constitution that would make subordinate certain governmental powers to the unalienable rights of men. Their thoughts and ideas put to paper is what gave rise to our Nation and each and every American should know this. Anyone who does not, has failed in their duty as an American. Future Americans cannot be expected to protect, defend and uphold something of which they have no understanding of.

Sadly, most Americans will never read our founding documents, either in part or in their entirety. They will learn only the little snippets given them by the revisionists of our day and will never be the wiser that certain political interests are counting on their ignorance. The Left in cahoots with academia and teachers unions across America, have already seen to it that our founding documents—either in-full or in-part—no longer appear in the History and Social Studies books of our primary and secondary schools. Aside from the obvious brainwashing capabilities this affords them, the only other explanation I have found for this travesty, is that a bunch of malcontented multicultural dumbasses have somehow been offended by the greater accomplishments of white men.

It would seem that for some, it does not matter how accurate or great the work is when the work is the construct of Whitey. Though, I suspect that even if our founding documents had been written by some government defined minority group, the Left would still find some reason for discrediting them to further their socialist cause. Despite the Left's disregard for the truth, I still think that most Americans are proud of their Nation's past accomplishments, even the ones attributed to white men.

How liberals can so despise the very documents which recognize their rights to act like a bunch of idiots is a baffling thing. It's kind of like hating your parents as a teenager after they have agreed to let you borrow the car. The idea that our founding documents are irrelevant because they were written by white men over 230 years ago, or that their legitimacy should be challenged in light of cultural equivocation is shear stupidity. No less idiotic is the Left's other claim that they are relics of the past and thus unsuited for a modern-day America. Their thoughts are especially frightening when you consider that among their more radical elements, individual rights should always be subordinate to the desires of the collective.

In such an irrational world, you might ask—how does one live a rational life and what are we to do when confronted with the absurdity of the irrational? I have only one answer to both questions; never compromise that which you know to be true. The truth can always be found, as long as you are willing to think logically and for yourself. Though the non-thinking will counter with their usual stupidity that such an assertion is not practical, because progress cannot be made without compromise, do not hesitate in your response. Their assertion that all things in life are relative, including the truth, is not only a logical fallacy, but idiotic. Their subjective view that compromise is necessary, as it allows for an orderly society, is equally suspect, especially given the treatment of those who have chosen to compromise with them. Tell me, just what was it that America gained in all those compromises on education, taxes and spending?

Let's suppose for one moment that they are correct and that compromise begets order and progress. Now let's consider the ramifications of such an argument in these three fields of study: mathematics, science and philosophy. We could take any field of study to discredit their argument, but I will use these as they allow for simple illustrations. It is necessary to keep it as simple as possible when dealing with the liberal mind so that they may be capable of understanding, as logic so often escapes them.

In the field of mathematics, let's assume for the moment that I have made the assertion that $2 + 2 = 4$, and my liberal antagonist has countered that $2 + 2$, in fact $= 5$. Following a heated discussion, neither of us is able to convince the other of the correct answer. It would appear that the rules governing mathematics were no more convincing to him, than his diatribe on the humanity of socialism and a new five year plan was convincing to me. Upon further discussion we then decide to compromise and meet in the middle, agreeing that $2 + 2$ must therefore equal 4.5. As you can plainly see, that in the end neither of us is correct and now both of us will suffer the consequences of our agreed upon stupidity.

The world is full of examples as to the dire consequences of compromise in the field of science. Take the latest Space

Shuttle disaster; we now know that the foam which broke away from the Shuttle's rocket booster and damaged the tiles of the left wing was due to the use of an inferior bonding agent. Why was the lesser product used? Well, it seems that concerns by environmentalists over the affects of the once used superior product, was enough to force NASA engineers to choose an inferior product as its replacement. It must be comforting to the families of the lost shuttle members to know that an inferior product won out over the safety of the crew.

Because of an unnecessary environmental compromise, we suffered the loss of seven astronauts and billions of dollars to appease environmentalists more concerned with the worship of Gaea, the goddess of Mother Earth, than those seven American heroes. How nice, I'm sure the spotted owl is very happy today and that Gaea will now look favorably upon her loyal idiot subjects. Anyway, radical environmentalists were not the first idiots to get in the way of science; 16th Century astronomer Galileo had to contend with his own nut-jobs.

Prior to Galileo it was generally accepted that the Earth was at the center of the Universe and that all heavenly bodies revolved around it. Though Galileo was not the first to speculate that the Sun was at the center of the Universe and that all planets revolved around it, he was the first to scientifically prove the theory. But since Galileo's proof went against church doctrine, it would be another two hundred years or so before his theory would be accepted.

Although the Catholic Church thought his theory to be blasphemous, Galileo never stopped in his quest to prove the theory first postulated by Copernicus. But what if he had? Of course it is pure conjecture, but where do you suppose astrophysics or any of the life sciences might be today had he compromised with the Vatican and ceased with his research? I'm sure someone else would have eventually figured it out, but is it not true that all technological progress is built upon yesterday's advancements. To disagree, one would have to believe that the personal computer would have been possible without the typewriter first being invented or that the automobile would have been made possible without the horse drawn carriage having been invented first.

Let's now consider the affects of compromise in the legitimate world of philosophy. Had the Founding Fathers surrendered their belief in individual liberty to King George or at the very least had they agreed upon a compromise, where do you suppose America would be today? First of all, there would never have been "The Declaration of Independence" much less "The Constitution of The United States". Had either of these documents never existed, would it be commonly accepted in America that each man has a right to "Life, Liberty and the Pursuit of Happiness?" Would any future government have ever recognized the same unalienable rights enumerated in the Bill of Rights? When you consider that even today, America is the only country to have done so, probably not.

Initially led by our example, France had its own revolution 13 years after the American Revolution, but chose not to accept or recognize the same unalienable rights of men. Since then, France has had numerous constitutions and still lacks the stability necessary to mature and develop as a respectable industrialized nation. Contrary to their smug feelings of superiority—based on what appears to be the work of artists long since dead—France to this day suffers from nothing short of an inferiority complex, one not unlike that of the Muslim states. Envy for the U.S. has become so entrenched in French society that one might consider it a national past-time.

Judging by France's history, envy for others may be a cultural thing, as they always seem to be in the unenviable position of wanting to be someone else. Why even during the 1936 Olympic Games held in Berlin, their athletes felt it necessary to lower the French flag to Hitler and present him with the Nazi salute. Many French were even undecided on who they would support during World War II. Would it be the Nazis, who just invaded and killed thousands of their fellow countrymen, or the Allies? Gee, that must have been a really tough one for them.

France's ties with Germany were so close that some were even complicit with Hitler and his henchman in their manner of dealing with the Jewish people. It is no secret that the Vichy government of France imprisoned and returned thousands of Jewish escapees to Germany. So, we shouldn't be at all surprised that they refused to support us in Iraq; it seems to be in their nature to side with those they fear. Their actions certainly make you wonder whether their attitude towards America would even be an issue today, had they adopted a similar Constitution.

From just the few examples I've given, you can imagine the dire consequences a false compromise can have on our lives. No leap of faith or stretch of the imagination is needed to realize that liberals have become to logic and reason what radical Islam is to individual thought and innovation. Much like their communist predecessors and their anti-American brothers around the world; the Left has shown that they will go to any extreme possible to quash dissenting opinion in their quest for power. In their quest for the same, neo-cons have proven too, that they're no lackeys either when it comes to limiting individual freedom.

If you have learned nothing from what I have written and are still asking the question; "Who are you to define what it is to be an American?" I'll give you the short, simple, and honest answer: nobody. This answer is not an attempt at modesty either, as I have never nor will I ever seek to humble myself before any leftist or anti-American sort. I have only answered the question as anyone would be required. Because the question should not be "who" defines what it is to be an American, but rather "what" defines what it is to be an American!

To be a true American one must adhere to a concrete set of principles. These principles are no secret as they have been clearly spelled out in our Nation's founding documents. Being a citizen of the United States may be enough to make you an American by law, but it by no means, is enough to make you a true American. Yes, it is every bit of my contention that being born in America does not make you fully American. That right has to be earned. Contrary to leftist doctrine there is an American culture and it is one based on the philosophy of Individualism.

It is because of this philosophy that when I am asked with impunity by the Left, whether I believe our founding documents, written over 200 years ago, are as relevant today as they were when they were written that I always answer:

"You're damn right I do!"